MODERN ENGLISH

exercises for
non-native speakers

PART I:
parts of speech

MARCELLA FRANK

New York University

PRENTICE-HALL, INC., Englewood Cliffs, New Jersey

ISBN: 0–13–593806–6

Printed in the United States of America

10   9

PRENTICE-HALL INTERNATIONAL, INC., *London*
PRENTICE-HALL OF AUSTRALIA, PTY. LTD., *Sydney*
PRENTICE-HALL OF CANADA, LTD., *Toronto*
PRENTICE-HALL OF INDIA PRIVATE LIMITED, *New Delhi*
PRENTICE-HALL OF JAPAN, INC., *Tokyo*

Contents

4

Auxiliaries   **85**

7

Adverbs 163

Preface

The purpose of the two volumes of *MODERN ENGLISH: Exercises for Non-native Speakers* is to provide advanced students of English as a foreign language with much carefully controlled and integrated practice on points of usage that continue to trouble such students. While the emphasis of these exercises is on written work, many of them may be used for oral drill as well.

The exercises are arranged systematically for ease of location. They progress from the less difficult to the more difficult, from strict control to looser control. Explanations are kept to a minimum; students understand what they are to do from the examples, many of which are given in contrast.

It would be desirable to use the workbooks in conjunction with *MODERN ENGLISH: A Practical Reference Guide*, which describes in detail the facts of usage on which the practice in the workbooks is based. However, the exercises have been set up so that the workbooks can be used independently of the reference guide.

The chapters in the workbooks are correlated with the chapters in the reference book. Thus, the sequence of practice moves from usage connected with the parts of speech to usage connected with the complex syntactic structures. As in the reference guide, the chapters on parts of speech have been influenced by structural grammar, those on complex syntactic structures by transformational grammar.

Part I: Parts of Speech

Each chapter on a part of speech begins with a chart outlining the structural features of the part of speech (function, position, form, markers). This outline is based on the description in *MODERN ENGLISH: A Practical Reference Guide*. Then come many exercises on word forms (inflectional and derivational suffixes, spelling peculiarities and irregularities), word order and other troublesome usages connected with each part of speech.

Part II: Sentences and Complex Structures

The complex structures that have been chosen for practice are those derived from simple basic sentences. Mastery of these structures is especially important for writing since they provide grammatical shapes for the expression of predications and thus relate grammar to meaning. The structures that are included are clauses, verbals, abstract noun phrases, and appositive phrases.

Each chapter on the complex structures is introduced by a chart that illustrated the various types of the structure. This is followed by transformational exercises involving: a) changes from the basic subject-verb-complement; b) the position(s) of the structure; c) the punctuation of the structure; d) substitutions for the structure; e) abridgment of the structure. At the end of each chapter is an exercise requiring a one-sentence summary of a paragraph.

After the student has done the intensive work offered in these workbooks on the correct use of words and sentences, he will have mastered the first stages of writing and should be ready for work in writing paragraphs and compositions.

I wish to acknowledge my special indebtedness to Milton G. Saltzer, Associate Director of the American Language Institute, New York University, for making it possible for me to try out a preliminary edition of these workbooks for several semesters at our Institute. Thanks are also due to my colleagues for their useful suggestions and comments, and to the students of the American Language Institute for helping me see which exercises needed improvement or change.

Marcella Frank
New York, New York

1

Nouns

STRUCTURAL DESCRIPTION OF NOUNS

Function	Sentences	Position
1. subject of verb	*John loves Mary.*	before the verb
2. object of verb		after the verb
a. direct object	*John loves **Mary**.*	
b. indirect object	*John sent **Mary** money.*	
c. retained object	*Mary was sent some **money**.*	
3. object of preposition	*I took it from **John**.*	after a preposition
4. complement		after the verb
a. subjective (after verbs like **be**)	*John is the **president**.*	
b. objective	*They elected John **president**.*	
5. Noun adjunct	*John waited at the **bus** stop.*	before a noun
6. appositive	*John, **president** of his club, gave a speech.*	after a noun
7. direct address	***John,** come here.*	usually at the beginning of the sentence

Form		Markers

Inflectional Endings
  -s for plural
 	
  's or *s'* for
  possessive
	Derivational Endings
	  -ment; -ion;
	  -a(e)nce;
	  -ure; -age;
	  -th; -ness;
	  -hood; -ship;
	  -ity; -ing
	
	  for a person
	  who: **-er; -or;**
	  -ist; -ant; -ian
		Determiners:
		The _____ (articles)
		My _____ (possessive)
		This _____ (demonstrative)
		Four _____ (number)
		Some _____ (indefinite pronoun)
		
		Descriptive adjectives:
		Large _____
		
		Prepositions:
		In _____
		Other nouns:
		Bus _____

FUNCTION OF NOUNS

A noun is the head word of the grammatical structure in which it functions.

Subject	*The **house** on the corner belongs to my uncle.* (**House** is the head word of the subject **the house on the corner**.)
Object of verb: direct object	*My husband sells expensive Chinese **antiques**.* (**Antiques** is the head word of the direct object **expensive Chinese antiques**.)
indirect object	*My uncle sold that rich **couple** some expensive antiques.* (**Couple** is the head word of the indirect object **that rich couple**. Indirect objects are used after verbs like **bring, buy, give, make, owe, pay, sell, send, teach, write**.)
Object of preposition: (in a prepositional phrase)	*The price of those **antiques** is very high.* (**Antiques** is the head word of the object of the preposition **those antiques**. Some common prepositions are **in, of, on, at, by, for, about, from, to, after**.)
Complement:[1] subjective complement	*My uncle is the richest **man** in town.* (**Man** is the head word of the subjective complement **the richest man in town**. Subjective complements appear after verbs like **be, seem, appear, remain, become**.)
objective complement	*I consider my uncle a very fortunate **man**.* (**Man** is the head word of the objective complement **a very fortunate man**. Objective complements are used after verbs like **appoint, consider, elect, name, nominate, select, choose**.)

Underline each noun in the following sentences and write its function above it—subject, direct or indirect object of verb, object of preposition, subjective or objective complement. Use the abbreviations S, DO, IO, OP, SC, OC.

1. All the children in that family have bad manners.

2. The customer sent the store a letter complaining about the service.

3. Her daughter was the only student in the school who won a prize.

4. The first President of the United States was George Washington.

5. The American people elected George Washington President.

6. The old man paid the boy some money for the newspaper.

---

[1]The word *complement*, in its broadest sense, also includes the object of the verb. In its narrowest sense it refers to the subjective complement only.

7. The company considers Mr. Jones the best man for the job.

8. Her son became a famous musician because of her encouragement.

1-2
PLURAL FORMS OF NOUNS

Nouns are regularly made plural by the addition of *s*. A number of nouns have other plural forms.

1. *es plural*
   a. nouns ending in sibilant sounds spelled with *s, z, ch, sh, x* — **classes, churches, dishes, boxes** *but* **monarchs** (*ch* spells a [k] sound)
   b. nouns ending in *y* preceded by a consonant: *y* is changed to *i* — **ladies, countries, boundaries** *but* **toys, keys** (*y* is preceded by a vowel)
   c. one-syllable nouns ending in a single *f* or *fe*: *f* is changed to *v* — **leaves, thieves, knives** but **sheriffs, staffs, beliefs, chiefs** Some words may also have a regular plural— **scarfs** *or* **scarves, dwarfs** *or* **dwarves.**

   d. nouns ending in *o*:
      es only — **Negroes, heroes, echoes, potatoes, tomatoes, embargoes**
      s only — terms in music—**pianos, sopranos** *o* preceded by a vowel—**cameo, radio** others—**photos, zeros**

      es or *s* — **cargoes** *or* **cargos, volcanoes** *or* **volcanos, mulattoes** *or* **mulattos**
2. *other types of plural*
   a. *-en* ending — **children, oxen, brethren**[2]
   b. internal vowel change — **teeth, mice, men**
   c. no change — **deer, sheep, series**

Write the plural for the following nouns. Use the dictionary where necessary.

apology _____   ox _____

businessman _____   fox _____

sheep _____   mosquito _____

bush _____   salmon _____

Negro _____   torch _____

quantity _____   embargo _____

tariff _____   species _____

---

[2]An older plural for **brother**, now used mainly in religious or literary contexts.

dash _____   story _____

attorney _____   memento _____

hero _____   quiz _____

wharf _____   supply _____

valley _____   epoch _____

means _____   studio _____

thief _____   bus _____

volcano _____   fallacy _____

arch _____   wife _____

1-3
FOREIGN PLURALS OF NOUNS

Singular ending	Plural ending	
-us	-i	stimulus—stimuli, radius—radii
-a	-ae	larva—larvae, vertebra—vertebrae
-um	-a	memorandum—memoranda, stratum—strata
-is	-es	crisis—crises, parenthesis—parentheses
-on	-a	criterion—criteria, phenomenon—phenomena
-ex, -ix	-ices	vortex—vortices, matrix—matrices
-eau	-eaux	bureau—bureaux, plateau—plateaux

There is a tendency for foreign words adopted in English to develop regular plural forms. Thus dictionaries now also give **memorandums**, **criterions**, **bureaus**.

Write the plurals of these foreign words that have been taken over into the English language. Note which of these words also have regular plural endings. Use the dictionary where necessary.

criterion _____   minutia _____

axis _____   stratum _____

alumna _____   cactus _____

alumnus _____   nebula _____

datum[3] _____   bacterium[3] _____

index _____   vertebra _____

chateau _____   syllabus _____

thesis _____   focus _____

formula _____   appendix _____

hypothesis _____   emphasis _____

1-4
INFLECTED POSSESSIVE FORMS

1. Use *'s* for all nouns not ending in *s*.
   a. *singular nouns*—The **girl's** dress is expensive.
   b. *irregular plurals of nouns*—The **children's** dresses are expensive.
2. Use **'** for all nouns already ending in *s*.
   a. *plural nouns*—The **girls'** dresses are expensive.
   b. *singular nouns, especially proper nouns*—**Dickens'** (*also* **Dickens's**) novels are excellent.
3. Use *'s* at the end of a group of nouns—The **Queen of England's** throne; the **boy from Canada's** mother.

The inflected possessive form is generally preferred for words referring to animate beings, the **of** phrase for words signifying things or ideas. However, the inflected form may also be used with nouns that represent: time (**a day's journey**), natural phenomena (**the earth's atmosphere**), political entities (**Japan's industrialization**), aggregates of people working together (**the company's new refinery**).

Change the **of** phrases in the following sentences to inflected possessive forms.

EXAMPLE: a. The parents *of the students* were invited to the graduation.
   The students' parents were invited to the graduation.
   b. It has always been the policy *of this newspaper* to report the news honestly and accurately.
   It has always been this newspaper's policy to report the news honestly and accurately.

1. The house *of Mr. Jones* has recently been sold.

_____

2. The crew *of the ship* decided to go on strike.

_____

---

[3]These words are rarely used in the singular.

3. He was irritated by the attitude *of his friends.*

_____

4. The rays *of the sun* shine on all.

_____

_____

5. The hunters are now on the trail *of the deer.*

_____

6. The doctor is waiting for the report *of the X-ray technician.*

_____

7. The distance *of the earth* from the moon is now known.

_____

8. The unwillingness *of the two countries* to negotiate their differences may lead to warfare between them.

_____

_____

9. The reputation *of this railroad* for safety and reliability has brought about its prosperity.

_____

_____

10. The hair *of the baby* is becoming lighter.

_____

11. People are not deceived for long by the outrageous lies *of that woman.*

_____

_____

1-5

COUNTABLE vs. NONCOUNTABLE NOUNS

Some nouns are not used in the plural. Such noncountable nouns may be:

1. *mass nouns* (representing concrete objects in their undivided form)
   a. foods—**sugar, coffee, milk, chicken, meat, fish**
   b. metals, minerals, gases, etc.—**gold, iron, coal, oil, oxygen, sulphur**
2. *abstract nouns* (including fields of study, sports)—**democracy, beauty, philosophy, chemistry, tennis.**

Add -*s* to the countable nouns that may be made plural.

information _____ ⎯ _____   vegetation _____ ⎯ _____

literature _____   youngster _____ s _____

vocabulary _____ ies _____   lumber _____ ⎯ _____

advertising _____   stationery _____ ⎯ _____

advertisement _____ s _____   luggage _____ ⎯ _____

climate _____ s _____   laughter _____ ⎯ _____

homework _____ ⎯ _____   traffic _____ ⎯ _____

assignment _____ s _____   knowledge _____ ⎯ _____

slang _____ ⎯ _____   mankind _____ ⎯ _____

weather _____ ⎯ _____   scenery _____ ⎯ _____

clothing _____ ⎯ _____   architect _____ s _____

machinery _____ ⎯ _____   engineering _____ ⎯ _____

machine _____ s _____   technology _____ ⎯ _____

propaganda _____ ⎯s _____   architecture _____ ⎯ _____

equipment _____ ⎯ _____   skyscraper _____ s _____

baseball _____ ⎯ _____   committee _____ ⎯ _____

Some nouns may have either a countable or a noncountable sense.

1. In their countable use, the nouns refer to individuals in a mass rather than to the mass itself.
   There were many *chickens* in the yard. (Chickens refers to the individual birds.)
   vs.   **They eat *chicken* very often. (Chicken** is considered in the mass—as one undivided item of food.)
2. The nouns used in a countable sense have the meaning of *a kind of*.

   The two most common *metals* for kitchen utensils are aluminum and stainless steel. (Metals implies *kinds of*.)

Use the noncountable singular noun or the countable plural noun. Do not use an article with the singular noncountable noun.

EXAMPLE: a. It has been said that (youth) _____ youth _____ is wasted on young people.
b. Several (youth) _____ youths _____ were loitering in the schoolyard.

1. The most expensive wigs are made of human (hair) _____ hair _____.
2. He is so bald that we can almost count the (hair) _____ hairs _____ on his head.
3. Various (fruit) _____ s _____ were on display at the fair.
4. Let's have some (fruit) _____ for dessert.
5. He has always been praised for his great (strength) _____ of (character) _____.
6. One of his great (strength) _____ s _____ is his ability to get along with people.
7. He doesn't like to drink (wine) _____ or (beer) _____.
8. France produces many (wine) _____ s _____.
9. That company will not hire you unless you have some (experience) _____.
10. He told about some of the terrible (experience) _____ s _____ he had had in the war.

1-6
DERIVATION (1)
ADDING AGENT-DENOTING SUFFIXES

Add noun suffixes to the following. Make whatever changes are necessary.

A. A person who _____ -s :
(Use *-or, -er, -ist, -ent*)

collect _____   discover _____

depend _____   invent _____

employ _____   sail _____

perform _____   tour _____

supply _____   farm _____

visit _____   reside _____

type _____   manage _____

conquer _____   advise _____

B. A person who is active in (or engages in) the field of _____ :
(Use *-ian, -ist, -eon, -er, -eer*)

biology _____ dentistry _____

music _____ engineering _____

chemistry _____ optometry _____

physics _____ auctioning _____

surgery _____ statistics _____

economics _____ writing _____

law _____ geology _____

1-7
DERIVATION (2)
CHANGING THE STEM BEFORE NOUN SUFFIXES

Fill in the blanks with the appropriate noun forms.

Nouns from Verbs

1. The (maintain) _____ of that building is the responsibility of Mr. Jones.
2. He gave a vivid (describe) _____ of his home town.
3. The child was punished for his (disobey) _____.
4. They built an (extend) _____ to the house.
5. His (succeed) _____ in business was the result of hard work.
6. The doctor gained immediate (recognize) _____ for his great discovery.
7. Everyone would like a (reduce) _____ in taxes.
8. We must find a (solve) _____ to this problem.
9. His wife's constant (suspect) _____ of infidelity irritated him.
10. The judge's (decide) _____ is final.
11. The tornado caused a great deal of (destroy) _____.
12. That gas can easily cause an (explode) _____.
13. What is the (pronounce) _____ of this word?
14. The (omit) _____ of a few words in the contract caused a great deal of trouble.

15. A (compare) _____ between the two systems reveals that one is much more efficient than the other.

16. For a long time people had many (misconceive) _____ about the nature of mental disorders.

17. He couldn't give a satisfactory (explain) _____ for his absence.

18. The girl's father asked her suitor what his (intend) _____ were in regard to marriage.

19. The (conquer) _____ of England by the Normans occurred in 1066.

Nouns from Adjectives

1. Cats and women have a great deal of (curious) _____.

2. What is the (deep) _____, the (high) _____ and the (long) _____ of this box?

3. Although he was a world-renowned scientist, he always behaved with (humble) _____.

4. He has great (strong) _____ and (noble) _____ of character.

5. He was thanked for his great (generous) _____.

1-8
DERIVATION (3)
DOUBLING FINAL CONSONANTS
BEFORE NOUN SUFFIXES

one-syllable word			rób	b	er
two-syllable word	*but*	oc préf	cúr er	r	ence ence

Note that: (1) the added noun suffix *begins with a vowel*; (2) the syllable before the noun suffix ends in a *single consonant preceded by a single vowel*; (3) the syllable before the added noun suffix is *stressed*.

Use the correct form of the noun.

1. The (propel) _____ of the plane was damaged.

2. Venus is the (god) _____ of love.

3. They had a large (wed) _____.

4. The (begin) _____ of the book is interesting.

5. He removed the (wrap) _____ from the candy bar.

6. We are writing in (refer) _____ to your letter of June 18.

7. There were many (beg) _____ on the road.

8. An (occur) _____ such as this was completely unexpected.

9. They traveled with very little (bag) _____ .

10. This ball is made of (rub) _____ .

11. There is a great (differ) _____ between the two brothers.

12. The chief argument for capital punishment is that it acts as a (deter) _____ to crime.

13. I'll ask the (drug) _____ what to take for my cold.

14. The police are taking measures to prevent the (recur) _____ of any violence by the strikers.

15. The (commit) _____ is deliberating that matter now.

1-9
DERIVATION (4)
ADDING NOUN SUFFIXES
TO WORDS THAT END IN SILENT *E*

1. **Keep the *e* before a consonant**

arrangement	Exceptions: judgment	wisdom
rudeness	acknowledgment	truth
statehood	abridgment	width
	argument	

2. **Drop the *e* before a vowel**

   purity
   creation
   composure

Add the designated noun suffixes to the words given below. Make whatever changes are necessary.

associate + ion _____

enclose + ure _____

advertise + ment _____

encourage + ment _____

expose + ure _____

wide + th _____

civilize + ation _____

operate + ion _____

judge + ment _____

idle + ness _____

interfere + ence _____

seize + ure _____

retire + ment _____

write + er _____

responsible + ity _____   polite + ness _____

receive + t _____   argue + ment _____

abridge + ment _____   safe + ty _____

scarce + ity _____   hostile + ity _____

1-10
DERIVATION (5)
CHANGING *Y* TO *I*
BEFORE A CONSONANT OR A VOWEL

y before a vowel: carriage   *y* before a consonant: happiness
                      supplier   loneliness
                      alliance   classification

Add the designated noun suffixes to the words given below. Make whatever changes are necessary.

bury + al _____   vary + ety _____

apply + cation _____   lovely + ness _____

marry + age _____   lively + hood _____

try + al _____   lazy + ness _____

holy + ness _____   likely + hood _____

sleepy + ness _____   busy + ness _____

1-11
DERIVATION (6)
CHANGING VERBS OR ADJECTIVES TO NOUNS

Fill in the noun form that is required because of the preceding italicized word.

EXAMPLE: He was greatly *attracted* by wealth, an _____attraction_____ which grew with the passing of years.

1. He soon became *acquainted* with the mayor, an _____ which brought him many political benefits.
2. The young boy was *grateful* to the judge for his leniency. His _____ took the form of helping other youngsters to obey the law.

3. He *hated* the kind of work he was doing. This _____ for his work finally caused him to resign from his job.

4. The old woman *longed* to see her son again. Her _____ was increased after she received a letter from him.

5. He was *not certain* that his farm could continue to be profitable. Because of this _____ he decided to sell the farm.

6. He was always severely *critical* of his wife. Finally his wife left him when she could no longer stand his _____ .

7. Their father was *partial* to the youngest daughter, a _____ that distressed the other children.

8. Many of the citizens were *indignant* because of the increase in taxes. They expressed their _____ by sending a lengthy petition to the mayor.

9. There is a saying that gentlemen *prefer* blondes. This _____ is probably not true for all gentlemen.

10. She always felt *inferior* to her beautiful sister. This feeling of _____ caused her to be shy and retiring.

11. Marcel Proust *remembered* many incidents of his childhood. This _____ of the past was all minutely recorded in his novels.

12. The wealthy young man decided to *renounce* his life of ease and become a hermit. This _____ of his former way of life surprised all his friends.

13. No one may *enter* through this gate. The _____ to the park is around the corner.

14. The heavy pack he was carrying *hindered* his movements. The camper decided that the next time he would take along nothing that would be such a _____ to him.

15. He *injured* his foot while climbing. This _____ prevented him from going any further.

16. When people are not *admitted* in a certain area, they will usually see a sign reading "No _____ ."

1-12

AGREEMENT WITH VERBS (1)

The verb must agree with the subject in number.

The **girl is** resting.
The **girls are** resting.

If the subject includes modifiers, the verb agrees with the noun head in the subject.

His **technique** for solving crimes **is** very simple.
The **advertisements** in the front part of a newspaper **are** usually the most expensive.

A noncountable noun used as a subject requires a singular verb.

His **baggage was** lost yesterday. (vs. His **bags were** lost yesterday.)
This **information is** correct. (vs. These **facts are** correct.)

A collective noun used as a subject generally occurs with a singular verb in American English, unless emphasis is to be placed on the individual members of the collective unit.

The committee has been preparing a new proposal.

but   The committee have disagreed among themselves about the terms of the proposal.

Some collective nouns always take a plural verb—*police*, *majority*, *minority*.

Put parentheses around the entire subject of each sentence, and underline the word that the verb agrees with. Then fill in the proper form of the verb. *Use only the present tense.*

EXAMPLE: a. (The rays of the sun) [shine] _____ shine _____ on all.
    b. (A little knowledge) [be] _____ is _____ a dangerous thing.

1. The amount of space between the lines (depend) _____ s _____ on the size of the story.

2. His method of doing things (be) _____ is _____ always admirable.

3. The choir (practice) _____ practices _____ twice a week.

4. An overuse of slang words (mark) _____ a person as uneducated.

5. Some members of the committee (be) _____ absent.

6. The public (be) _____ invited to attend the meeting.

7. Many people on the ship (be) _____ getting seasick from the violent waves.

8. The singing of the birds (awaken) _____ me every morning.

9. The police (be) _____ patrolling that area very carefully.

10. The clothing on these racks (be) _____ being put on sale tomorrow.

11. The front page articles in that newspaper usually (consist) _____ of news about international events.

12. No frozen poultry (be) _____ sold in this store.

13. A sound knowledge of mathematics (be) _____ required for this kind of work.

14. The number of people who understand Einstein's theory of relativity (be) _____ very small.[4]

15. A number of people (be) _____ waiting at the airport to greet the movie star.

16. The spirit in which these things are done (be) _____ very important.

[4]**The number** is usually singular, **a number** plural.

1-13

AGREEMENT WITH VERBS (2)
NOUNS ENDING IN *S*

Some nouns ending in *s* may cause problems in agreement.

1. Some are singular noncountable nouns—**news, measles** (name of a disease), **economics** (name of a field of study)—

    The news about the war is not good; Physics is a difficult subject.

    The name used for a field of study may be plural if it refers to a practical matter—

    The acoustics in this room are not good.

2. Some nouns have the same form for *singular or plural*—**series, means, species.**
3. Some nouns are plural only and require *plural verbs*—**brains, riches, goods, clothes.**
    Included in this group of plurals are nouns signifying two-part objects—**scissors, trousers, eyeglasses.** A few nouns of this type are sometimes also used with singular verbs—**headquarters, barracks.**
4. Nouns representing quantities and amounts that are considered as one unit are singular—**five dollars, three quarts.**

    Five dollars is too much to pay for that pen.

Underline the correct form of the verb. Consult the dictionary in case of doubt about whether the noun ending in *s* is singular or plural.

1. Mathematics (has, have) never been my favorite subject.
2. The news printed in that paper (is, are) never accurate.
3. A second series of books on American literature (is, are) being planned by the publisher.
4. There (is, are) several means of accomplishing our purpose.
5. The scissors (was, were) here a few minutes ago.
6. Over $1,500 (has, have) already been withheld from his salary for federal income taxes.
7. Billiards (is, are) his favorite game.
8. Two gallons of paint (is, are) all we need.
9. The goods (was, were) shipped yesterday.
10. Athletics (has, have) always been emphasized in this school.
11. The mumps (causes, cause) a swelling of the glands below the ears.
12. The proceeds of the sale (is, are) going to charity.
13. Ten minutes (is, are) too short a time to finish this test.
14. The premises of the school (has, have) been cleared of students because of a bomb threat.
15. His ethics in that business deal (is, are) being questioned by some financial experts.

AGREEMENT WITH VERBS (3)
NOUNS FROM ADJECTIVES

Adjectives used as nouns often refer to a group of persons and require a plural verb. Such adjective forms are usually preceded by **the**.

The Scotch have the reputation of being thrifty.
The rich get richer, while the poor get poorer.

Change each of the phrases beginning with **those who** to **the** + **an adjective**. Then supply the correct form of the verb **be**.

EXAMPLE: Those who were seriously wounded (past) immediately taken to the hospital.

The seriously wounded were immediately taken to the hospital.

(Note that an adjective used as a noun may retain its adverbial modifier—*seriously*.)

1. *Those who are aged* (present) now being provided with cheap or free medical care.

---

2. *Those who are young* (present) often very impatient with their elders.

---

3. *Those who were talented* (past) encouraged to enter their paintings in the contest.

---

4. *Those who are needy* (present) now receiving enough to live on.

---

5. *Those who are unemployed* (present) entitled to apply for unemployment insurance.

---

6. Only *those who were very prominent* (past) invited to the reception.

---

7. After the terrible landslide that destroyed the village, *those who were living* (past) removed at once, *those who were dead* (past) left behind.

---

8. In this school, *those who are blind* (present) being taught Braille, *those who are deaf* (present) being taught how to speak.

---

9. *Those who were the most aggressive among the strikers* (past) in favor of prolonging the strike.

_____

10. *Those who are socially acceptable* (present) the only ones who are ever invited to their home.

_____

2

Pronouns

STRUCTURAL DESCRIPTION OF PRONOUNS

Function and Position	Inflectional Form

Personal Pronouns

Similar to those of nouns. See p. 1	*Subject*	*Object*	*Possessive Adjective*	*Possessive Pronoun*	*Reflexive*
	I	me	my	mine	myself
	you (s.)	you	your	yours	yourself
	he	him	his	his	himself
	she	her	her	hers	herself
	it	it	its		itself
	we	us	our	ours	ourselves
	you (pl.)	you	your	yours	yourselves
	they	them	their	theirs	themselves

neutral reflexive—oneself *or* one's self

Interrogative and Relative Pronouns

who	whom	whose	whose

Demonstrative Pronouns

singular	*plural*
this	these
that	those

Note that the possessive form of personal pronouns are written without an apostrophe (**its, ours**, etc.).

Types of Pronouns

1. Personal—**I, you, he, she, it, we, they**

2. Interrogative—**who, what, which**

3. Relative—**who, which, that**

4. Demonstrative—**this, that, such, so**

5. Reflexive—compounds of personal pronouns plus **-self**

6. Indefinite:
   a. persons or things—compounds of **some-, any-, no-,** or **every-** plus **-body, -one, -thing**
   b. quantity—**some, any, several, much,** etc.

   (Personal, relative, demonstrative, reflexive pronouns refer back to nouns previously mentioned.)

7. Expletive—**it, there** (These words fill subject position. The actual subject comes after the verb.)

2-1
FORM OF PERSONAL PRONOUNS

Use the correct form of the pronoun in parentheses. Give the function of each pronoun—subject (**s**), subjective complement (**sc**), object of verb—direct or indirect (**ov**), object of preposition (**op**), appositive (**a**).

EXAMPLE: a. John and (I) _____ I _____ are the same age. _____ S _____ .

b. The only two who were absent were John and (I) _____ I _____ .
_____ SC _____ (after the verb **be**)

c. Our teacher praised John and (I) _____ me _____ . _____ OV _____

d. The letter was addressed to John and (I) _____ me _____ .
_____ OP _____

e. (We) _____ We _____ girls are planning a picnic. _____ A _____
(appositive to the subject)

1. The money was given to (he) _____ and (I) _____ .

_____

2. Their mother is taking (they) _____ all to the circus.

_____

3. Everyone finished the test except (I) _____ . _____

4. All of (they) _____ came late. _____

5. My sister and (I) _____ are arriving on the early train.

_____

6. (We) _____ children were spoiled by our parents.

_____

7. Between (you) _____ and (I) _____ ,
she's not very happy in her new home. _____

_____

8. It was (I) _____ who planned this meeting. _____

9. Hello, may I speak to Mrs. Jones?
This is (she) _____ . _____

10. They wanted only Robert and (I) _____ . _____

11. (She) _____ and her sister are planning to give a dinner party together. _____

12. Who's at the door?
It's (I) _____ .[1] _____

2-2
POSSESSIVE FORMS OF PRONOUNS

Supply one of the possessive forms of the personal pronouns or of **who**. Be careful not to write an apostrophe with any of these pronouns.

EXAMPLE: a. He didn't bring a coat, so I lent him (I) _____ mine _____ .
   b. The store is opening (it) _____ its _____ doors one hour earlier today.
   c. (Who) _____ Whose _____ book is this? I don't know (who) _____ whose _____ book it is.

1. The cat caught (it) _____ tail in the door.[2]

2. In (who) _____ house will the meeting be held?

3. The man (who) _____ car was stolen went to the police immediately.

4. Every nation has (it) _____ own special problems.

5. Can you tell me which house is (they) _____ ?

6. The earth rotates around (it) _____ axis every 24 hours.

7. I don't remember whether the pen I borrowed is (he) _____ or (she) _____ .

8. Whether the fault is (they) _____ or (we) _____ , we must correct it immediately.

9. Here are some papers. (Who) _____ are they? Are they (you) _____ ?

10. The children who are making so much noise are (we) _____ .

11. (Who) _____ money was used to finance the deal?

---

[1]Although formal usage requires subject form for such a subjective complement, the object form is more common in informal speech.

[2]The forms of **he** and **she** are also often used for pets.

2-3
DOUBLE POSSESSIVE CONSTRUCTIONS
WITH PRONOUNS

Personal pronouns may appear in double possessive constructions beginning with of—**an old hat of yours, a casual acquaintance of mine.**

Use a double possessive construction for the pronouns in parentheses.

EXAMPLE: a. He is a good friend (I) _____ of mine _____.
           b. Some students (her) _____ of hers _____ were on a TV discussion program.
           c. That car (they) _____ of theirs _____ always gave them trouble.

1. Any friend (you) _____ is a friend (I) _____.

2. An old classmate (he) _____ is coming to dinner.

3. A neighbor (us) _____ likes to gossip a great deal.

4. I can understand why they're so proud of that son (they) _____.

5. A good customer (he) _____ died recently.

6. Some papers (you) _____ got mixed in with some notes (I) _____.

7. Almost no friends (they) _____ came to the funeral.

8. Many patients (he) _____ stopped coming to him after he raised his fees.

9. Those jade carvings (they) _____ are worth a fortune.

2-4
WHO vs. *WHOM*

Who is the subject form, **whom** the object form. (In informal usage, **who** is often also used for the object of a verb.)

Who or **whom** appears in direct questions, in indirect questions (noun clauses), and in adjective clauses.

In the following exercises, supply **who** or **whom**. (Observe formal usage.) Label each pronoun you have filled in—Subject (**s**), Object of Verb (**ov**), Object of Preposition (**op**).

Direct Questions

EXAMPLE: a. _____ Who _____ is watering the plants? _____ S _____
           (of **is watering**).
           b. _____ Whom _____ do you want? _____ OV _____ (of **do want**)
           c. From _____ whom _____ did he receive the money? _____ OP _____ (of **from**)

1. _____ are they discussing?
   _____

2. To _____ did they deliver the flowers?
   _____

3. _____ was given the instructions?
   _____

4. _____ can they be sending us?
   _____

5. _____ will volunteer to do this job?
   _____

Indirect Questions (Noun Clauses)

EXAMPLE: a. I know _____ who _____ is watering the plants. _____ S _____
   (of **is watering**)
   b. I know _____ whom _____ you want. _____ OV _____
   (of **want**)
   c. I know from _____ whom _____ he received the money. _____ OP _____
   (of **from**)

1. We can't imagine _____ could have done such a thing.
   _____

2. They will soon announce _____ they have chosen.
   _____

3. Please let us know to _____ the money should be sent.
   _____

4. I can't remember from _____ I bought this. _____

5. The teachers tried to guess _____ might be appointed as
   the new principal. _____

Adjective Clauses

EXAMPLE: a. The man _____ who _____ is watering the plants is the gardener.
   _____ S _____ (of **is watering**)
   b. The man _____ whom _____ you want is the gardener. _____ OV _____
   (of **want**)
   c. The man from _____ whom _____ he received the money is the gardener.
   _____ OP _____ (of **from**)

1. The girl with _____ she is living is a brilliant student.
   _____

2. I always appreciate a person _____ can be trusted.
   _____

3. The woman _____ we hired as a cook will start tomorrow.
   _____

4. He is a man on _____ you can depend. _____

5. I don't know anyone _____ can do this job. _____

A reflexive pronoun generally *points back to the subject*. It is used:

1. as the direct object of the verb—**You mustn't blame *yourself* for that mistake.**
2. as the indirect object of the verb—**I bought *myself* a beautiful watch.**
3. as a prepositional object:
   a. of a verb—**We should depend on *ourselves* rather than on others.**
   b. of an adjective—**She's angry with *herself* for making such a mistake.**

Supply the required reflexive pronoun.

EXAMPLE: a. Albert Schweitzer dedicated _____ himself _____ to caring for the sick in Africa. (**Himself** is the direct object of the verb **dedicated**.)

   b. She made _____ herself _____ a dress. (**Herself** is the indirect object of the verb **made**.)

   c. He's very selfish; he thinks only about _____ himself _____. (**Himself** is the prepositional object of the verb **thinks**.)

   d. They are ashamed of _____ themselves _____. (**Themselves** is the prepositional object of the adjective **ashamed**.)

1. It's time I bought _____ a new car.

2. If we could only see _____ as others see us.

3. The children washed and dressed _____ quickly.[3]

4. She's quite pleased with _____ for finishing the job on time.

5. They built _____ a beautiful home.

6. Did both of you enjoy _____ at the party?

7. You should always depend on _____ rather than on someone else.

8. God helps those who help _____.

9. He's angry with _____ for misplacing the money.

10. You will all have to be responsible for _____.

11. They are always quarreling among _____.

12. He's telling a story about _____.

13. Try not to make a fool of _____.

14. They are constantly talking about _____.

15. We must now devote _____ wholeheartedly to the task at hand.

[3]The reflexive pronoun is optional in this sentence.

2-6
REFLEXIVE PRONOUNS AS INTENSIFIERS

Reflexive pronouns used as intensifiers are not necessary for the grammatical structure of a sentence. They merely serve to emphasize nouns or pronouns.

Intensifying a *subject*	We **ourselves** will lead the discussion. (= *we and no one else*)
or	We will lead the discussion *ourselves*. (*Final position is possible only if the sentence or clause is short.*)
	Shakespeare **himself** could not have said it better. (= *even Shakespeare*)
or	Shakespeare could not have said it better **himself**.
Intensifying an *object*	I saw the chief **himself**.
	They want us to lead the discussion **ourselves**.
	We spoke to the victims **themselves**.

Use a reflexive pronoun to emphasize each of the italicized words. If the italicized word is a subject, note whether the reflexive intensifier may also appear in final position.

EXAMPLE: a. The *governor* _____ himself _____ cannot help the condemned man.
——————————— —

    b. *You* _____ yourself _____ cannot believe such a thing. _____ yourself _____

1. Their unexpected success at the polls surprised the *candidates* _____.

2. This package must be given to the *president* _____.

3. *We* _____ must do the work. _____

4. *She* _____ had nothing to do with the robbery. _____

5. *He* _____ told us about the matter. _____

6. The report was written by *the department head* _____.

7. *The victims* _____ can't explain how the accident happened. _____

8. *You* (plural) _____ would not care to be put into such an unpleasant situation. _____

9. *The party members* _____ don't believe that their leaders are honest. _____

10. *The President* _____ gave instructions on what to serve for the state dinner. _____

11. Many people think he's a great man. *I* _____ once thought so _____, but I don't any more.

12. He _____ would never have permitted such a thing to happen _____; someone else must have planned it.

PRONOUNS FOR GENERAL STATEMENTS

Several pronouns may be used to represent people in general (generic person).

we	We all get into trouble sometimes.
they (*informal*)	They grow coffee in Brazil. (*more formal*—Coffee is grown in Brazil.)
	They say that honesty is the best policy. (*more formal*—It is said that honesty is the best policy.)
you (*informal*)	You have to study very hard at the university.
one (*formal*)	One should do one's (*or* his) duty in all things.
everybody *or* **everyone**	Everybody should obey the law.

In making general statements, we should not shift from one generic person to another.

Shift in person—If **we** are making statements about people in general, **one** should not from one person to another, but **you** should be consistent in **your** use of pronouns of generic person.

Corrected to—If **we** are making statements about people in general, **we** should not shift from one person to another, but **we** should be consistent in **our** use of pronouns of generic person.

A pronoun referring back to a noun which represents a class should have the same number as the noun.

Shift in number—The **student** must be made to understand how each lesson can be of value to **them**.

Corrected to—The **student** must be made to understand how each lesson can be of value to **him**. (**He** is used to refer back to a class word which includes both males and females.)

Fill in the blanks with the proper pronouns for general statements. Avoid a shift in person or number.

EXAMPLE: a. _____One_____ should always be careful when ____one (*or* he)____ is crossing the street.

or

_____Everybody (*or* everyone)_____ should always be careful when *he* is crossing the street.

b. _____They_____ say that the number thirteen is unlucky.

c. A teacher must be sure that all of _____his_____ students understand the point _____he_____ is making.

d. _____You_____ never really know what love is until _____you_____ experience it _____yourself_____ (reflexive).

or

_____We_____ never really know what love is until *we* experience it *ourselves*.

1. _____ all need to relax at times.

2. _____ should be loyal to the country _____ live in.

3. If a person practices typing every day, _____ can become an expert.

4. Doctors are responsible for the lives of _____ patients.

5. During the war everyone had to look out for _____ (reflexive).

6. _____ should not give up before _____ absolutely have to.

7. _____ should love _____ neighbors as _____ love _____ (reflexive).

8. _____ do things somewhat differently in every country.

9. Dentists say that _____ should brush _____ teeth every day.

10. The company expects _____ to do a full day's work.

11. _____ should not expect as much of others as _____ expect of _____ (reflexive).

12. _____ should try to keep _____ streets clean.

2-8
PRONOUNS WITH *-EVER*

The **-ever** forms of pronouns have several uses.

Intensifiers in questions	*Whatever* made you insult that man? *Whoever* told you to do such a thing?
Intensifiers in negatives (equivalent to **at all**)	He doesn't understand any English *whatever* (or *whatsoever*). (*Only these forms with **what** are negative intensifiers.*)
Alternatives for **no matter who—what—which**	*Whoever* knocks at the door, don't answer it.
Introductory words in noun clauses	*Whoever* broke the window must pay for it. Take *whatever* you want.

Supply **whoever, whatever,** or **whichever.**

EXAMPLE: a. Give this to one of the boys, _____whichever_____ one comes to the door first.

b. _____Whoever_____ gave you permission to leave the office early?

c. _____Whatever_____ happened to those nice people who used to live next door to you?

1. He will borrow money from _____ is willing to lend it to him.

2. I have no money _____.

3. _____ finishes first will win a prize.

4. I will abide by _____ decision you make.

5. He is very grateful to _____ helps him.

6. He tells the same story to _____ he meets.

7. _____ he does is done well.

8. We'll employ _____ woman the agency sends us.

9. He'll do _____ you say.

10. _____ he paints expresses his deep spirituality.

11. _____ marries her will be a lucky man.

12. _____ TV channel he turned on, he saw nothing but westerns or murder mysteries.

13. We know no one _____ in this town.

14. _____ she does displeases her husband.

15. _____ is worth doing at all is worth doing well.

2-9

AGREEMENT WITH INDEFINITE PRONOUNS (1)

Each, every, either, neither require singular verbs. Possessive (or other) pronouns referring to one of these words are singular in formal speech.

> **Each** student **is bringing his** lunch.
> (**His** is used if reference is made to a group of males and females together.)
> **Everyone is** expected to do **his** best.
> **Neither** of the girls **has** done **her** homework.

In *informal* usage, a plural verb may occur with **either, neither**; and a plural pronoun may refer to **each, every, either, neither**.

For each sentence, fill in the required form for the verb and the pronoun. Ue only the present tense. Observe formal usage.

EXAMPLE: a. Each of the boy scouts (be) _____ is _____ bringing _____ his _____ own camping equipment.
   b. All of the boy scouts (be) _____ are _____ bringing _____ their _____ own camping equipment.

1. Everyone (have) _____ _____ own way of doing things.

2. Each of the awards (be) _____ for a large sum of money.

3. Either of the women (be) _____ willing to lend you _____ vacuum cleaner.

4. Each employee (be) _____ being asked to contribute as much as _____ can.

5. Everybody in the office (seem) _____ pleased with the raise _____ has received.

6. Neither of the lamps (be) _____ suitable for this table.

7. Both of the lamps (be) _____ suitable for this table.

8. Each student (be) _____ requested to ask
_____ parents to come to the parents-teachers association meeting.

9. Either you or I (be) _____ mistaken.[4]

10. Every apartment in the building (need) _____ some
repairs.

2-10
AGREEMENT WITH INDEFINITE PRONOUNS (2)

A pronoun of indefinite quantity like **some**, **all**, **none**, **most** plus an **of** phrase
requires a verb that agrees with the *noun in the* **of** *phrase*.

Some of the **machines need** to be repaired.
Some of the **machinery needs** to be repaired.

The same rule applies if words that refer to a part (**half, rest, remainder**) or
a fraction (**one third, three fourths**) are used.

Half of the **pie was** eaten.
Half of the **pies were** eaten.

Use the required form of the verb **be**.

EXAMPLE: a. All of her jewelry (*past*) _____ was _____ put in a safety vault.
b. All of her jewels (*past*) _____ were _____ put in a safety vault.

1. None of the pies (*past*) _____ eaten.[5]

2. None of the dessert (*past*) _____ eaten.

3. All of the information on the report (*present*) _____
correct.

4. All of the statistics on the report (*present*) _____ correct.

5. Most of his luggage (*past*) _____ lost on his last trip.

6. Most of his bags (*past*) _____ lost on his last trip.

7. Some of that poet's work (*present*) _____ very fine.

8. Some of that poet's works (*present*) _____ very fine.

9. Most of the merchandise (*present perfect*) _____ sold.

10. Most of the goods (*present perfect*) _____ sold.

11. All of this fruit (*present*) _____ from their garden.

12. All of these apples (*present*) _____ from their garden.

13. Half of the turkey (*present*) _____ for today's dinner.

[4]In formal usage, the verb agrees with the noun or pronoun after (n)or.
[5]Some conservative handbooks claim that only a singular verb should be used with **none**.

14. Half of the dinner guests (*past*) _____ staying with their hosts overnight. The remainder (*past*) _____ taking the last train back to town.

15. Almost one third of the people in the world (*present*) _____ always hungry.

2-11

EXPLETIVE *THERE* vs. EXPLETIVE *IT*

Expletive **there** commonly occurs in the following types of sentences.

1. **There** + **be** + (pro)noun + *expression of place*

> There's nobody **here.**
> There's a piano **in the room.**

2. **There** + **be** + noun with *adjective modifiers*

> There was once **a very wicked** king.
> There are **three** reasons **for rejecting that proposal.**

3. **There** + **be** + noun + *—ing participle*

There is a sale **going on** at the bookstore. (= A sale is going on at the bookstore.)
There is a strong wind **coming up** from the west. (= A strong wind is coming up from the west.)

In a sentence with expletive **there,** the verb agrees with the actual subject that follows it.

> There **is** a **book** on the desk.
> There **are** some **books** on the desk.

Expletive **it** is often found in the following constructions.

1. **It** + **be** + adjective + *adverbial construction*

> It's gloomy **here.**
> It's pleasant **in the garden.**
> It would be wise **if you went there now.**

2. **It** + **be** + an expression of:

identification	What is this? It's *a lawn mower.*
weather	It's *cold* outside.
time	It's *Wednesday* (*or ten o'clock, January 25*).
distance	It is *five miles from the library to my house.*

Only a singular verb is used with expletive **it.**

Supply **it is, there is, there are.**

EXAMPLE: a. _____It is_____ raining outside now.
b. _____There is_____ no place like home.
c. _____There are_____ many simple recipes in this cookbook.

1. _____ more comfortable over here.

2. _____ someone waiting in the office to see you.

3. Who is at the door? _____ Mary.

4. _____ two good reasons why you shouldn't go there.

5. _____ not a house to be seen for miles around.

6. _____ very warm today.

7. _____ many books on man-made satellites in the library.

8. _____ too cold to go outside.

9. What time _____? _____ a quarter past two.

10. _____ a lot of changes that should be made.

11. _____ more efficient if you do it this way.

12. _____ snowing very hard now.

13. _____ more births than deaths in some countries.

14. _____ many ways of telling a lie.

15. _____ only one way of telling the truth.

16. _____ often very windy near the ocean.

17. _____ some people who are never satisfied.

18. _____ no fool like an old fool.

19. _____ so hot that we can't work.

20. What is this? _____ a vacuum cleaner.

21. _____ something wrong with this typewriter.

22. _____ enough books for everyone in the class.

23. _____ too noisy here for us to study.

24. _____ too much noise here for us to study.

25. _____ a few pages missing from today's newspaper.

2-12
ANTICIPATORY *IT*

An anticipatory **it** construction is used to avoid having a long noun structure appear in subject position. The construction without anticipatory **it** is felt as a more formal one.

Change each sentence so that it begins with **it**.

IT with Infinitive Phrase Subject

EXAMPLE: a. To take a drive in the country is very pleasant.
It is very pleasant to take a drive in the country.
b. For me to do that is quite difficult.
It is quite difficult for me to do that.

1. To fill out all these forms is very time-consuming.

_____

2. To take some exercise every day is good for the health.

_____

3. To speak before a large audience takes a great deal of self-assurance.

_____

_____

4. For man to land a space ship on the moon is now possible.

_____

5. To become a good doctor requires much training and experience.

_____

_____

6. For him to work so hard makes no sense.

_____

7. To speak English well is difficult for foreign students.

_____

_____

IT with THAT Noun Clause Subject

EXAMPLE: That he should resent such a remark is natural.
It is natural that he should resent such a remark.

1. That he will never be a success is becoming evident.

_____

2. That he was able to sell that old car of his was a surprise to us.

_____

_____

3. That we will never finish on time is becoming apparent.

_____

4. That he failed his examinations is a shame.

_____

5. That he might be very ill never occurred to me.

_____

6. That no one came to the airport to greet him disappointed him.

_____

_____

7. That she couldn't have her way frustrated her.

_____

3

Verbs

STRUCTURAL DESCRIPTION OF VERBS

Function—The verb is the grammatical "center" of the sentence.

Position—The verb appears after the subject and before any type of complement in the predicate. (See position of nouns.)

Form—The verb has three regular inflectional endings—-s, -ed, -ing. Auxiliaries are also used with verbs to form *verb phrases*. The one-part verbs and the verb phrases that may function as verbs in the predicate are:

Tense	Active Voice		*Progressive*	Passive Voice				*Progressive*
Present	offer*, offers*		am / is / are } offering	am / is / are } offered		am / is / are } being offered		
Past	offered*		was / were } offering	was / were } offered		was / were } being offered		
Future	will / shall } offer		will / shall } be offering	will / shall } be offered				
Present perfect	have / has } offered		have / has } been offering	have / has } been offered				
Past perfect	had offered		had been offering	had been offered				
Future perfect	will / shall } have offered		will / shall } have been offering	will / shall } have been offered				

*These auxiliary-less verbs are called the *simple* present and the *simple* past.

The auxiliaries **can—could, may—might, must, would, should** also help to form the verb in the predicate. The forms of verb phrases used with these auxiliaries are:

Present		*Past*		*Perfect*	
can may must	offer	could might should would	offer	could may—might should would	have offered

Progressive		*Passive*	
can—could may—might should would	be offering	can—could may—might should would	be offered

3-1
ADDING INFLECTIONAL ENDINGS

Add **-s** (third person singular), **-ed** (past tense), and **-ing** (present participle) to the following verbs.

	-s	-ed	-ing
Verbs with Final -y or -ie			
study	studies	studied	studying
marry			
hurry			
liquefy			
carry			
worry			
play	plays	played	playing
employ			
convey			
enjoy			
display			
die	dies	died	(*irreg.*) dying
tie			(*irreg.*)
lie (*recline*)		(*irreg.*)	(*irreg.*)
lie (*tell an untruth*)			
Verbs with Final -e			
advise	advises	advised	advising
change			
dine			
continue			

	-s	-ed	-ing
write		(*irreg.*)	
argue			
shine		(*irreg.*)	
lose		(*irreg.*)	
agree	agrees	*agreed*	agreeing
guarantee			
free			
see		(*irreg.*)	

Verbs with Final Single Consonants Preceded by Single Vowels

	-s	-ed	-ing
plán	pláns	plánned	plánning
dróp			
whíp			
bég			
contról	contróls	contrólled	contrólling
permít			
occúr			
prefér			
regrét			
equíp			
trável	trávels	tráveled (*U.S.*) trávelled (*Brit.*)	tráveling (*U.S.*) trávelling (*Brit.*)
wórship			
cáncel			
équal			
tótal			
bénefìt	bénefìts	bénefìted	bénefìting
intérpret			
devélop			

Verbs with Final Sibilants (Spelled -s, -z, -ch, -sh, -x)

	-s	-ed	-ing
push	pushes	pushed	pushing
guess			
quiz			
watch			
teach		(*irreg.*)	
ambush			
fix			
buzz			
crush			

Change the following nouns to verbs by adding the suffixes **-en, -ize, -ify**. Make whatever changes are necessary.

apology _____   memory _____

fright _____   solid _____

character _____   satire _____

beauty _____   strength _____

author _____   standard _____

haste _____   terror _____

critic _____   threat _____

class _____   sympathy _____

emphasis _____   colony _____

liquid _____   glory _____

length _____   summary _____

drama _____   symbol _____

height _____

3-3
DERIVATION (2)
ADDING PREFIXES *EN-*, *BE-*, *AC-*, *IM-*

Change the following nouns to verbs by adding the prefixes **en-, be-, ac-, im-.**

custom _____   knowledge _____

friend _____   slave _____

joy _____   prison _____

head _____   title _____

circle _____   witch _____

climate _____   trust _____

force _____   courage _____

3-4
DERIVATION (3)
CHANGING NOUNS TO VERBS

In the blank spaces supply the verbs that are related to the italicized nouns. Use the correct verb forms.

1. The *production* of coal in our country is very great. How much coal does your country _____ ?

2. It is so easy to see through his *pretenses*. Why must he always _____ to be more important than he is?

3. The *applause* was deafening. There was no one in the room who was not _____ loudly.

4. If he won't take my *advice*, why did he ask me to _____ him?

5. His ultimate *success* depends on how well he _____ in every step along the way.

6. The *explosion* was heard for miles around. No one knew what had caused the airplane to _____ .

7. It's time for the baby's *bath*. Would you like to _____ him?

8. The *loss* of life was very great in the last war. In the next war we may _____ many more men than we _____ in the previous war.

9. I'm all out of *breath*. It's difficult to _____ in this high altitude.

10. His *choice* of words was unfortunate. Sometimes it's important to _____ the right words. In his place, I would have _____ words that were not so emotional.

11. Nostradamus made many *prophecies*. He _____ that the world would be destroyed in the year 2000.

12. The kind of *proof* you have offered does not _____ conclusively that you are right.

13. He may _____ other people, but I can see right through his *deception*.

3-5
IRREGULAR VERBS (1)

The tense forms of a number of verbs differ from the regular forms. The principal parts of such verbs must be known before the proper tense forms can be used. The first principal part of a verb is the *simple form of the verb* (the infinitive without **to**), the second principal part is the *past tense*, the third principal part is the *past participle* (used for the perfect tenses or for the passive forms). Thus, the principal parts for the regular verb **offer** are—**offer, offered, offered**.

The exercises that follow are grouped according to the kind of irregularity the verbs show.[1] Supply the proper verb forms for the past tense; then change each sentence to the present perfect, using an appropriate time expression for this tense (**just, already, so far, up to now, always, never, sometimes, this morning, etc.**)

All Three
Principal Parts are Different

sing, sang, sung

begin, drink, ring, shrink (past also shrunk), sing, sink, swim

EXAMPLE: I (begin) _____ began _____ the work yesterday.
I have already begun the work. _____

1. They (drink) _____ too much beer yesterday.

_____

2. The bell (ring) _____ a few minutes ago.

_____

3. We (sing) _____ Christmas carols last night.

_____

4. The ship (sink) _____ some time ago.

_____

break, broke, broken

break, choose, freeze, steal, speak, weave

5. Our club (choose) _____ a new president last month.

_____

[1] A list of irregular verbs is given in the appendix in alphabetical order.

6. The bank robber (steal) _____ the money the day before yesterday.

7. They (freeze) _____ the food before they shipped it.

drive, drove, driven   drive, ride, (a)rise, write

8. He (drive) _____ too fast last night.

9. She (ride) _____ a beautiful white horse when she was young.

10. We (write) _____ the letter yesterday.

11. The sun (rise) _____ at six this morning.

In the following exercises you may omit the time words, but keep in mind that the past tense represents *definite* past (**yesterday, last year, a week ago**), while the present perfect represents *indefinite* past.

blow, blew, blown   draw, fly, grow, know, throw, withdraw

EXAMPLE: The artist (draw) _____ drew ; has drawn _____ the picture.

12. The boys (throw) _____ pennies into the well.

13. The helicopter (fly) _____ over the city.

14. The boy (grow) _____ very fast.

wear, wore, worn   bear (past participle borne and born)[2], swear, tear, wear

15. He (swear) _____ to get revenge.

16. She (bear) _____ her troubles without complaint.

17. His wife (wear) _____ her new gown to the ball.

[2]**Borne** is the usual past participle of **bear** in all uses except with **be**. **Be born** represents the fact of birth—**She was born in France.**

bite, bit, bitten

bite, chide (also chided, chided), hide

18. The dog (bite) _____ the boy.

19. He (hide) _____ the money under the bed.

shake, shook, shaken

forsake, mistake, shake, take

20. He (forsake) _____ his wife for another woman.

21. I (mistake) _____ you for an acquaintance.

22. They (take) _____ the wrong train.

Other Verbs Whose Principal Parts are All Different

be	was	been
do	did	done
eat	ate	eaten
fall	fell	fallen
go	went	gone
lie	lay	lain
see	saw	seen
(a)wake	(a)woke	(a)waked, *British* (a)woke *or* (a)woken
	sometimes (a)waked	

23. He (do) _____ the work very efficiently.

24. She (eat) _____ her dinner too fast.

25. The girl (fall) _____ on the ice.

26. They (go) _____ to the park.

27. He (lie) _____ in bed all day.

28. I (see) _____ a good movie.

29. They (be) _____ in the country for three weeks.

30. We (awake) _____ in time to see the sun rise.

3-6
IRREGULAR VERBS (2)

Supply the verb forms for the past tense and the present perfect tense.

Second and Third
Principal Parts are Alike

hang, hung

cling, dig, hang[3], sling slink, spin, stick, sting, strike[4], string, swing, wring

EXAMPLE: A bee (sting) _____ stung; has stung _____ him in the arm.

1. She (hang) _____ the clothes on the line.

2. They (dig) _____ a hole for the tree.

3. He (stick) _____ the notice on the bulletin board.

4. The pendulum (swing) _____ back and forth.

feed, fed
   or
creep, crept

bleed, breed, feed, flee, lead, speed

creep, dream[5], feel, keep, kneel[5], leap[5], leave, mean, meet, sleep, sweep, weep

5. He (mean) _____ what he said.

6. The snake (creep) _____ along the ground.

7. He (feed) _____ his dog twice a day.

8. The refugees (flee) _____ from their pursuers.

9. He (keep) _____ his money in the safe.

10. The captain (lead) _____ the men.

11. She (meet) _____ her husband-to-be at a party.

12. She (sweep) _____ the dirt under the rug.

[3]When **hang** refers to death by suspension by the neck, the past tense as well as the past participle is **hanged.**

[4]**Stricken** is the past participle of **strike** when used figuratively as an adjective—**conscience-stricken, terror-stricken, stricken with a disease.**

[5]These verbs also have the regular alternatives **dreamed, kneeled, leaped.**

bring, brought   beseech, bring, buy, catch, fight,
                                                        seek, teach, think

13. We (think) _____ you were in trouble.

14. The boy (catch) _____ a cold.

15. They (fight) _____ a losing battle.

16. The secretary (bring) _____ her lunch with her.

17. Her mother (teach) _____ her how to sew.

bend, bent   bend, lend, rend, send, spend

18. He (spend) _____ too much money for that car.

19. She (lend) _____ her neighbor her vacuum cleaner.

20. The strong wind (bend) _____ the tree.

bind, bound   bind, find, grind, wind

21. The butcher (grind) _____ the meat.

22. I (find) _____ a watch in the street.

23. The doctor (bind) _____ the wound with a clean bandage.

pay, paid   lay, mislay, pay, say

24. He (mislay) _____ the report.

25. They (pay) _____ all their bills.

sell, sold   sell, tell

26. They (sell) _____ their car.

Other Verbs Whose Second and Third Principal Parts are Alike

abide (*literary*)	abode
build	built
clothe	clad (*literary*) (*also* **clothed**)
forget	forgot (*or, past participle* **forgotten,** *American usage*)
get	got (*or, past participle* **gotten,** *American usage*)
have	had
hear	heard
hold	held
behold (*literary*)	beheld
withhold	withheld
light	lit[6]

[6]Also, **lighted,** meaning *to provide light,* or as an adjective (**A well-lighted room**).

lose	lost
make	made
shine	shone[7]
shoe	shod
shoot	shot
sit	sat
slide	slid
stand	stood
understand	understood
withstand	withstood
tread (*literary*)	trod (*or, past participle* **trodden**)
win	won

27. I (hear) _____ the news on the radio.

28. He (hold) _____ many important positions.

29. The policeman (shoot) _____ the robber.

30. I (forget) _____ to mail the letter.

31. He (lose) _____ money in the stock market.

32. The men (withstand) _____ the fierce attack by the enemy.

33. He (win) _____ some money at the horse races.

34. The sun (shine) _____ very brightly.

All Three
Principal Parts are Alike

bet (sometimes **betted** for the past tense and the past participle)	let
	put
bid (meaning *offer money at an auction*)	read
broadcast (sometimes **broadcasted** for the past tense and the past participle)	rid
	set
burst	shed
cast	shut
cost	slit
hit	spit (sometimes **spat** for the past tense and the past participle)
hurt	
knit (also **knitted** for the past tense and the past participle)	split
	spread
	thrust

35. The boy (hit) _____ the dog.

36. The radio (broadcast) _____ the President's entire speech.

37. He (shut) _____ the door.

[7] **Shined** is used for the transitive verb—**The boy shined his shoes.**

38. The pipes (burst) _____ because of the cold.

39. His carelessness (cost) _____ him his life.

40. She (spread) _____ the butter on the bread.

First and Third
Principal Parts are Alike

come	came	come
become	became	become
overcome	overcame	overcome
run	ran	run

41. He (overcome) _____ all difficulties.

42. The children (run) _____ away.

First and Second
Principal Parts are Alike

beat   beat   beaten (or **beat**)

43. He (beat) _____ the dog with a stick.

3-7
IRREGULAR VERBS (3)

Use the **past tense** (second principal part), or the **past participle** (third principal part) of the irregular verbs in parentheses.

EXAMPLE: a. Many planes (fly) _____ flew _____ over this village a few minutes ago. (past tense)

b. She has (wear) _____ worn _____ her new dress only once. (past participle after the auxiliary **have**)

c. The window was (break) _____ broken _____ some time ago. (past participle after the auxiliary **be** with a passive verb)

1. I fell asleep just as soon as I (lie) _____ down on the bed.

2. No one knows where the robbers have (hide) _____ the money.

3. The girl (fall) _____ off the horse yesterday and (hurt) _____ herself badly.

4. I have (see) _____ several good movies this year.

5. The clothes were (hang) _____ on the line to dry.

6. It was (think) _____ that he had met with an accident.

7. The money was (lend) _____ to him by a friend.

8. All the bills were (pay) _____ yesterday.

9. The apartment house was (build) _____ ten years ago.

10. Our team (win) _____ the game yesterday.

11. The same car (cost) _____ $100 less a year ago.

12. She doesn't remember where she (lay) _____ the packages yesterday.

13. Construction on the building was (begin) _____ three years ago.

14. He didn't get up until long after the sun had (rise) _____.

15. The picture was (draw) _____ by a famous artist.

16. He (swim) _____ so far out from shore that the lifeguard signaled for him to come back.

17. A hole has already been (dig) _____ for the well.

18. He was (strike) _____ in the face by a baseball.

19. What is (mean) _____ by this word?

20. She has (bring) _____ two of her children with her.

21. We seem to have (lose) _____ our way.

22. The money was (put) _____ in the bank right away.

23. He has (lie) _____ in bed all day.

24. He was (choose) _____ to lead the men.

25. He has (drive) _____ many racing cars.

26. Her coat was (tear) _____ on a nail.

27. The boy was (bite) _____ by a mosquito.

28. Several notes were (stick) _____ up on the wall.

29. This tray was (buy) _____ at Woolworth's.

30. The holdup victim was (shoot) _____ in the arm.

31. He has already (sleep) _____ for ten hours.

32. The suspected thief is being (seek) _____ by the police.

33. She has always (dream) _____ of being a ballerina.

34. The watch has already been (wind) _____ today.

35. She (weave) _____ the rug on her own loom.

36. The child (cling) _____ fearfully to her mother.

37. She (weep) _____ uncontrollably when she heard of her friend's death.

38. The announcement was (read) _____ to all the members.

39. The robber (bind) _____ his victim to a tree.

40. The dictator is such a tyrant that many people have (flee) _____ from the country.

SIMPLE PRESENT TENSE
vs. PRESENT PROGRESSIVE TENSE

Simple present	*Present progressive*

1. expresses *repeated action* (includes the past, present and future)
The earth revolves around the sun. (general truth)
I go there very often. (custom)
	1. expresses *one action in the present*
	  a. of short duration
	    He's studying the lesson.
	    He's writing a letter.
	  b. of long duration
	    He's studying English.
	    He's writing a book.

2. expresses *non-action* (state or condition) **He seems tired.** **She loves her children.** **I remember him.** **I hear some music.** (vs. **I am listening to some music.**)	2. expresses *future action* **He's giving a lecture tomorrow.** **The ship is sailing next week.**
3. expresses *future action* (especially with verbs of arriving and departing) **We leave tomorrow.** **The ship sails next week.**	3. expresses the beginning, progression or end of an action **It is beginning to snow.** **My cold is becoming worse.**

Supply the simple present or the present progressive form of the verb. In a few sentences either form may be used.

EXAMPLE: a. The milk (taste) _____ tastes _____ sour.

      b. She (taste) _____ is tasting _____ the soup to see if it needs more salt.

      c. The wind (blow) _____ is blowing _____ very hard outside.

1. The play (begin) _____ now.
2. She (try) _____ to finish her work early today.
3. It (get) _____ colder and colder.
4. I (hope) _____ to see you again.
5. We (plan) _____ to buy a house soon.
6. Children (learn) _____ faster when they are interested in what they (study) _____.
7. We (go) _____ to the movies tonight.
8. The sun (rise) _____ in the east and (set) _____ in the west.
9. I sometimes (forget) _____ to take my keys when I (leave) _____ the house.
10. She (take) _____ a nap every afternoon.
11. I (hear) _____ some loud noises outside.
12. He (listen) _____ to the radio.
13. I (see) _____ some children outside.

14. I (watch) _____ the children play outside.

15. We (understand) _____ now why he was so angry.

No ing 16. I (believe) _____ he will be here soon.

No ing 17. He (admire) _____ his father very much.

18. We (be) _____ are _____ short of paper; we (need) _____ some more.

19. He (say) _____ says _____ he can do it for you.[8]

20. She (consider) _____ is _____ entering the university.

21. He (write) _____ is _____ a book on Africa.

22. What (you think) __ are _____ about?

23. What (you think) __ Do _____ of the new plan?

24. All the students (have) __ are _____ a good time at the party.

25. At present he (live) __ is or lives _____ in California.

26. You (waste) _____ are _____ your time doing it that way.

27. Many people (enjoy) _____ enjoy _____ going to the beach.

28. He (spend) __ is _____ this week at the beach; he (enjoy) __ is _____ himself very much.

29. Americans (celebrate) _____ Independence Day on July 4.

30. She always (interfere) _____ in other people's affairs.[9]

31. She (spend) _____ too much money on clothes.

32. He (stay) _____ at a very luxurious hotel.

33. Water (boil) _____ at 212 degrees Fahrenheit and (freeze) _____ at 32 degrees.

3-9

SIMPLE PAST TENSE
vs. PAST PROGRESSIVE TENSE

Both forms of the past tense represent *definite past*. They refer to events that were completed before the statement is made. They are often accompanied by such expressions of definite past as **yesterday, last year, two weeks ago**.

The past progressive emphasizes *duration of an action* in the past—**What were you doing all day yesterday?**. The past action may be of short duration—**What were you doing at ten o'clock last night?**

Use the simple or progressive form for the past tense. In some sentences both past tense forms are possible.

EXAMPLE: a. Just as he (reach) _____ reached _____ the bus stop, the bus (pass) _____ passed _____ by him.

b. He (work) _____ was working _____ in a restaurant the last time I (see) _____ saw _____ him.

---

[8]The simple present is often used for verbs of saying and telling.

[9]With **always, constantly, perpetually,** the progressive form of the verb may also be used.

1. The minute we (receive) _____ his gift, we (write) _____ him a note of thanks.

2. When they (hear) _____ the burglar alarm go off, they (call) _____ the police.

3. They (eat) _____ dinner in the cafeteria a few minutes ago.

4. At 7 o'clock last night I (eat) _____ dinner.

5. Everyone (enjoy) _____ himself at the party.

6. Shakespeare (write) _____ his great plays many years ago.

7. All last year he (prepare) _____ for the bar examination.

8. After the movie (be) _____ over, they (go) _____ to the restaurant for coffee.

9. Where is the dog? I (see) _____saw_____ him only a few minutes ago.

10. As soon as he (open) _____opened_____ the door, his son (run over) _____ran over_____ to greet him.

11. The guards quickly (catch) _____caught_____ the prisoner who (try) _____was trying_____ to escape.

12. She (cut) _____cut_____ her finger while she (prepare) _____was preparing_____ dinner.

13. When the teacher (walk) _____walked_____ into the classroom, the students (become) _____became_____ quiet.

14. They (leave) _____left_____ town some time last month.

15. We reached the lake just as the sun (set) _____was setting_____.

16. In Columbus' day, people (believe) _____believed_____ that the earth (be) _____was_____ flat.

3-10

PAST PROGRESSIVE TENSE

Wherever possible, change the verbs to progressive form. Keep in mind that the progressive emphasizes *duration of a single event.*

EXAMPLE: a. What did he think about my plan?
   (*no change possible*) _____

   b. She thought about the accident all night long.
   She was thinking about the accident all night long. _____

   c. The driver stopped the bus very quickly.
   (*no change possible*) _____

1. We watched television last night.

_____

2. They opened the new store last week.

_____

3. They borrowed some money from the bank.

_____

4. The telephone rang all day long.

_____

5. He got to the platform just as the train left.

He got to the platform just as the train was leaving

6. He counted his change several times before he left the store.

He counted his change several times before he left

7. At the party last night, people sang, danced, and ate.

singing   dancing   eating

8. At the beginning of the semester, we reviewed all of last year's work.

reviewing

9. The children played in the snow all afternoon long.

The were playing

10. The typist omitted a few words from the letter.

omitted

11. She held on to the child very tightly.

holding on

12. We were in the middle of the desert when we ran out of gas.

were   when we were running

13. They argued all evening long about who would win the election.

were arguing

14. It rained very hard last night.

was raining

15. They sat so close to the stage that they could observe every gesture of the performers.

were sitting

_____

PAST PROGRESSIVE WITH TIME CLAUSES

One continuous past action may be interrupted by a non-continuous past action.

She was washing the dishes when the phone rang.

The past progressive form is used for the continuous action.

A. Combine each set of sentences so that the *second sentence* becomes a **when** clause. Use the required verb forms.

EXAMPLE: I (cross) the street.
　　　　　I (see) an accident.
　　　　　I was crossing the street when I saw an accident.

1. She (do) her homework.
　　She (become) very sleepy.

_____

2. The refugees (walk) along the road.
　　Some planes (appear) overhead.

_____

3. She (prepare) dinner.
　　A quarrel (break out) among the children.

_____

4. They (eat) breakfast.
　　They (hear) someone knock at the door.

_____

5. She (put) some water in the coffee pot.
　　She (notice) a leak in the pot.

_____

6. The old gentleman (walk) in the park.
　　A man with a gun (approach) him.

_____

7. They (watch) television.
　　The lights (go out).

_____

8. The student next to me (daydream) in class.
　　The teacher (address) a question to him.

_____

9. The children (play) in the street.
A stranger (walk) over to them.

_____

10. The family (eat) dinner.
The telephone (ring).

_____

11. The hero (embrace) the heroine.
Someone in the theater (shout) "Fire".

_____

12. The orchestra members (get) ready to start the performance.
They (hear) some commotion in the rear of the concert hall.

_____

B. Many of the sentences of the form **I was doing something when something happened** may also take the form **While I was doing something, something happened.**

She **was washing** the dishes when the phone **rang.**

or While she **was washing** the dishes the phone **rang.**

Note that no matter which statement becomes the time clause, past progressive form is used for the continuous action.

As or **just as** may be alternatives for **while** in this kind of time clause.

Just as we were sitting down to dinner, the phone rang.

Combine the sets of sentences in A so that the *first sentence* becomes a **while** or **(just) as** clause.

EXAMPLE: While I was crossing the street, I saw an accident.

_____

3-12
FUTURE TIME

There are several ways to express future time.

future tense	auxiliary **will**—may be used for all persons auxiliary **shall**—used for the first person (considered formal usage in the United States) progressive future—used for a *single action* especially if it has duration
simple present tense	especially with verbs of arriving and departing—requires a future time expression
present progressive tense	used with many verbs expressing action
be going to	often adds the idea of *intention* or *expectation* to future time

For the following sentences, add the other ways of expressing future time.

EXAMPLE: a. The ship will sail tomorrow.

The ship will be sailing tomorrow. (future progressive)

The ship sails tomorrow. (simple present)

The ship is sailing tomorrow. (present progressive)

The ship is going to sail tomorrow. (**be going to**)

b. He will call you tomorrow.

He will be calling you tomorrow. (future progressive)

He is going to call you tomorrow. (**be going to**)

1. I will meet him later.

_____

_____

_____

_____

2. We will give a party tomorrow.

_____

_____

_____

_____

3. She will bake some cookies tonight.

_____

_____

_____

_____

4. They will return next week.

_____

_____

_____

_____

5. The play will begin at 7: 00 P.M. on Sunday evenings.

_____

_____

_____

_____

6. It will rain tonight.

_____

_____

_____

_____

7. I will need your help in a few minutes.

_____

_____

_____

8. The travel agency will plan our itinerary.

_____

_____

_____

9. He will go to work by bus next week.

_____

_____

_____

_____

10. The plane will arrive at 10: 00 o'clock.

_____

_____

_____

11. They will write us from London in a few days.

_____

_____

_____

_____

12. The store will close soon.

_____

_____

_____

_____

FUTURE PROGRESSIVE TENSE

Wherever possible, change the verbs to progressive form. Keep in mind that the future progressive form, like the present progressive, may refer to a single action that has very short duration.

1. I shall arrive tomorrow.

_____

2. He will get a raise in salary soon.

_____

3. She will pay me back next week.

_____

4. I will telephone him later tonight.

_____

5. He will be angry if you don't come.

_____

6. They will buy a house next year.

_____

7. My aunt will visit me soon.

_____

8. He will finish his book this year.

_____

9. That lawyer will give you some good advice.

_____

10. That trip will cost a lot of money.

_____

11. You will never forget that trip.

_____

12. I will help you wash the dishes.

_____

13. You will love her the moment you meet her.

_____

14. He will become rich.

_____

15. We will have more time later to do that.

_____

3-14
PRESENT PERFECT TENSE

The present perfect tense represents time that begins in the past and extends to the present, either in actual fact or in the mind of the speaker. It is not used with definite time words like *yesterday, last year*.

The kinds of time words that express past-to-present time are:

since *or* **for**	I have lived here for three years. *or* I have lived here since 1969.
so far, up to now, up to the present	We have had no trouble with our television set so far (*or* up to now).
frequency words—**always, never, ever, often, some-times, occasionally,** etc.	He has always lived in this town. This is the best book I have ever read.
just, already (negative **yet**), **finally**	Our dinner guests have just arrived.
recently, lately[10]	She has not seen him recently.

If no time word is given, either the past or the present perfect tense is possible, depending on whether the time is felt as definite past, or past to present.

Supply the correct forms of the present perfect tense. Do not use the progressive forms for this exercise.

EXAMPLE: a. Ruth (just return) _____has just returned_____ from South America.

         b. We (already have) _____have already had_____ breakfast.

    1. The professor (lecture) _____ for over an hour.

    2. They (know) _____ each other since childhood.

    3. (You ever taste) _____ such good apple pie?

[10]Informally, except for **since, for,** the past tense is often used with these time words that characterize past-to-present time.

4. He (still not realize)[11] _____ what a bad mistake he (make) _____ .

5. He is the worst student she (ever have) _____ .

6. The baby (sleep) _____ for three hours.

7. He (have) _____ many difficulties since he came to this country.

8. Some students (study) _____ all week for the examination, while others (not begin) _____ yet.

9. I (knock) _*have knocked*_ on the door for fifteen minutes, but so far no one (answer) _*has answered*_ .

10. The news about the war (not be) _*hasn't been*_ good lately.

11. His admirers (wait) _*have waited*_ in the rain for two hours just to see him get off the plane.

12. I (not see) _____ him since last winter.

13. He (recently arrive) _____ in this country.

14. I (never see) _____ such beautiful mountains.

15. He (already finish) _*has already finished*_ his first book and he (begin) _*has begun*_ to work on the second one.

16. I (visit) _____ that museum three times so far.

3-15

PRESENT PERFECT PROGRESSIVE TENSE

The present perfect progressive tense is generally used for a single action that extends from the past to the present. It is not used to express repetition, and it does not occur with the words **just**, **already**, **ever**, **never**, **finally**.

Wherever possible, change the present perfect verbs to progressive form.

EXAMPLE: a. She has gone to school off and on all her life.
     She has been going to school off and on all her life.

     b. He has seen a great deal of her lately.
     He has been seeing a great deal of her lately.

     c. I have seen that movie many times.
     (No change possible)

1. She has said the same thing for an hour.

_____

2. They have worked on that bridge all year long, but it is still not completed.

_____

[11]In the present perfect, **still** is used only with the negative. **Still** *precedes* the auxiliary.

3. The sick boy has not stayed in bed as the doctor ordered.

_____

4. All day long I have waited for the telegram to arrive.

_____

5. He has worked for the same company for 25 years.

_____

6. They have played tennis since early this morning.

_____

7. He has lived at that hotel a week now.

_____

8. She has watered the lawn for an hour.

_____

9. They have just spent three weeks at their country home.

_____

10. The tenants have finally paid the rent they owed.

_____

11. The landlord has promised to fix the leak in the ceiling for a long time.

_____

12. The same mailman has delivered the mail for ten years.

_____

13. The mailman has just delivered the mail.

_____

14. He has not felt well recently.

_____

15. The cost of living has risen steadily.

_____

16. Ever since I heard the news, I have wondered about it.

Ever since I heard the news, I have been wondering about it.

17. Has he ever written to you since he left town?

_____

PRESENT PERFECT TENSE
vs. PAST TENSE

Use the present perfect tense for indefinite time (with **since, for, often, so far, recently,** etc.), or the past tense for definite time (with **yesterday, a few days ago, last week,** etc.). Note where the progressive forms of the verb are possible or preferable.

EXAMPLE: a. He (live) _____*has lived, has been living*_____ in the same house since he was born.

b. A plane headed for the West Coast (crash) _____*crashed*_____ in the mountains last night.

c. Her husband (die) _____*died*_____ of a heart attack a few years ago.

1. He (not smoke) *has not been smoking* for several weeks.
2. We (always want) *have always wanted* to take a trip around the world.
3. The girl (fall) *has fallen* off her bicycle many times.
4. He (work) *worked* in a factory last summer to earn his tuition for the university.
5. He (be) *has been* a member of Congress for many years.
6. She (do) *has done* her exercises faithfully every day.
7. We (sell) *sold* our house several weeks ago.
8. Da Vinci, Michelangelo, Raphael (create) *created* great works of art during the Italian Renaissance.
9. There (be) *have been* many accidents on that road recently.
10. Many prominent people (be) *were* in the audience last night.
11. I (have) *have had* this toothache since yesterday.
12. He (attend) *has attended* the university until he ran out of money last year.
13. Because of the storm last night, they (cancel) *cancelled* all flights from the airport.
14. His business (prosper) *has been prospering* so far.
15. Emerson and Thoreau (write) *wrote* in the 19th century.
16. She (have) *had* the flu last month. She (not feel) *has not been feeling* well since.
17. Up to now we (never have) *I have never had* any trouble with our refrigerator.
18. I (not yet see) *have not yet seen* that play.
19. In the past, more people (live) *lived* on farms.
20. He (be) *has been* seriously ill for the past few days.

3-17
PAST PERFECT TENSE (1)

The past perfect tense expresses past time that precedes another past time.

The burglar alarm went off and a crowd began to gather. Soon the police arrived at the scene of the robbery. But they were too late. The thieves **had** already **gone**.

The past perfect tense often occurs in sentences containing dependent clauses.
1. *Adverbial clauses*

   The teacher took my paper before I had finished the test.
   After I had spoken, I realized my mistake.
   Although she had reported the theft immediately, the police were unable to help her.

2. *Adjective clauses*

   The man who had stolen the money two weeks ago confessed last night.
   The house where he had lived as a child was right on a lake.

3. *Noun clauses*

   He said that he had left his wallet at home.
   He was worried about what he had just heard.

In each of the following sentences, use a past perfect verb in one of the clauses, and a past verb in the other.

EXAMPLE: a. Before his mother (say) _____ had said _____ one word of reprimand, the child (begin) _____ began _____ to cry.

   b. Because she (not report) _____ had not reported _____ the theft immediately, the police (be) _____ were _____ unable to help her.

   c. They never (receive) _____ received _____ the books which they (order) _____ had ordered _____ .

1. Almost all the guests (leave) _____ had left _____ by the time we (arrive) _____ arrived _____ .

2. He (never be) _____ had never been _____ ill in his life until he (go) _____ went _____ into the jungle.

3. He (wonder) _____ wondered _____ whether he (leave) _____ had left _____ his wallet at home.

4. The company (not hire) _____ did not hire _____ him because he (lie) _____ had lied _____ about his past experience.

5. After a while he (realize) _____ realized _____ that he (take) _____ had taken _____ the wrong road.

6. The secretary (not leave) _____ did not leave _____ until she (finish) _____ had finished _____ her work.

7. The police (ask) _____ asked _____ the boy why he (steal) _____ had stolen _____ the money.

8. They (be married) ___had been married___ for five years before any friction (arise) ___arose___ between them.

9. When she (finish) ___had finished___ her work, she (go) ___went___ to the movies.

10. She (want) ___wanted___ to know what (happen) ___had happened___ at the meeting.

11. The weather (be) ___was___ far worse than we (expect) ___had expected___.

12. By the time we (get) ___got___ to the airport, our plane (already leave) ___had already left___.

13. The girl who (promise) ___had promised___ to baby-sit for them (be) ___was___ too ill to do so.

14. I (not know) ___didn't know___ that they (move) ___had moved___ back to their old home.

15. I (hear) ___heard___ many things about this country before I (come) ___had come___ here.

16. He (can) ___could___ still remember the good times he (have) ___had had___ as a child.

3-18
PAST PERFECT TENSE (2)
WITH *JUST, ALREADY*

In informal speech, the past tense is often used rather than the past perfect tense (**After I spoke, I realized my mistake; The man who stole the money two weeks ago confessed last night; He said he left his wallet at home**). However, in a sentence that contains a past time clause, a main verb accompanied by **just, already, scarcely, barely, no sooner** must be in the past perfect tense—**She had just washed the windows when it began to rain.**

Combine each group of sentences so that the second sentence becomes a **when** time clause.

EXAMPLE: a. We (just sit) down to dinner.
             A fire (break out) in the kitchen.
             We had just sat down to dinner when a fire broke out in the kitchen.

          b. He (scarcely begin) to work on his new job.
             He (become) seriously ill with pneumonia.
             He had scarcely begun to work on his new job when he became seriously ill with pneumonia.

1. He (just buy) a new home.
   His company (transfer) him to another city.

   _____

   _____

2. The examination (already begin).
They (discover) that one page of the examination paper was missing.

_____

_____

3. His daughter (just give up) hope that she could win in the contest.
She (receive) a telegram saying she had been awarded first prize.

_____

_____

4. The student (barely skim) through his new art book.
He (lose) it on the subway.

_____

_____

5. She (already put away) her winter clothes.
An unseasonable cold spell (force) her to take them out again.

_____

_____

6. The company (already ship) the merchandise.
They (realize) they had sent it to the wrong address.

_____

_____

7. He (barely overcome) one financial difficulty.
Another, more serious one (face) him.

_____

_____

8. She (just make up) her mind to attend a particular college.
She (receive) a scholarship from a more desirable school.

_____

_____

9. The couple (scarcely enter) the house.
They (begin) to argue.

_____

_____

10. They (no sooner sell) their car.
They (regret) having done so.[12]

_____

_____

11. They (just hire) a new cook.
The old one (ask) for her job back.

_____

_____

12. The car (hardly go) a mile.
It (have) a flat tire.

_____

_____

13. The guest speaker (no sooner enter) the hall.
A cheer (arise) from the audience.[12]

_____

_____

3-19
PAST PERFECT PROGRESSIVE TENSE

Wherever possible, change the verbs to progressive form. Keep in mind that the progressive usually emphasizes *duration of a single event*.

EXAMPLE: a. The actor who had played the part of Hamlet became too ill to go on stage.
The actor who had been playing the part of Hamlet became too ill to go on stage.

b. He had never missed a day's performance until he became ill.
(*no change*)

c. He said that he had studied for several hours.
He said that he had been studying for several hours.

1. He had worked for several hours when the mailman came with a special delivery letter.

_____

_____

2. They had discussed several important matters before I got there.

_____

_____

[12]In formal usage, **no sooner** requires a **than** clause rather than a **when** clause.

3. We had just sat down to dinner when the doorbell rang.

_____

_____

4. They told us that they had enjoyed their visit to their aunt.

_____

_____

5. They had planned for a long time to move to the suburbs.

_____

_____

6. Because he had always paid his bills regularly, the bank granted him a loan.

_____

_____

7. He had taken the X-ray treatments up to the time he left.

_____

_____

8. The people who had bought the house next to ours painted it a bright red.

_____

_____

9. They had lived in the slums for several years when I first met them.

_____

_____

10. He said that he had tried to reach us by phone all day long.

_____

_____

11. The store would not refund her money because she had removed the price tag.

_____

_____

12. The children fought for some time before their mother separated them.

_____

_____

3-20
FUTURE PERFECT TENSE

The future perfect tense expresses a future time that precedes another future time. This future-before-future time may actually *begin in the past*. The future perfect tense is usually accompanied by a time expression which signals *at*, *by*, or *before* which time a future event will be completed.

On the 10th of next month, she will have been a widow for two years.
At the end of this summer, I will (or shall) have been away from home for ten years.
When he retires from his work, he will have made more than a million dollars.
By the end of the school year, we will (or shall) have covered the entire grammar book.
Before his vacation is over, he will have made many new friends.

Fill in the blanks with the future perfect tense.

EXAMPLE: a. By the year 2000, this earth (see) _____ will have seen _____ many changes.

b. The taxi (arrive) _____ will have arrived _____ by the time we get downstairs.

1. By the time the rehearsal is over, the audience (begin) _____ to enter the theater.

2. By next year, he (forget) _____ everything he learned in this class.

3. By the time he is an old man, he (lose) _____ many of his youthful ideals.

4. Next month they (be) _____ in the United States for thirty years.

5. Before he leaves New York, he (go) _____. to every museum in town.

6. By the end of the semester, your English (improve) _____ tremendously.

7. By December, all the leaves (fall) _____ from the trees.

8. On the 26th of this month he (complete) _____ his tour of Europe.

9. By the time you get there, they (rehearse) _____ for ten hours.

10. The political prisoners (escape) _____ from the country by the time their absence is noticed.

11. The leaders of the present regime (help) _____ themselves to a great part of the treasury before they are forced out of power.

12. In ten years time we (pay) _____ off the mortgage on our house.

13. By the time he leaves Las Vegas, he (lose) _____ a great deal of money at the gambling tables.

3-21
PASSIVE FORM OF VERBS (1)

Many verbs may be used to make statements about the same event in two different ways.

Active voice   The boy (*subject*) opened the door (*object*).

Passive voice   The door (*original object*) was opened by the boy (*original subject*).

Because an original object becomes the grammatical subject in a passive statement, *only transitive verbs*[13] *may be used in the passive voice.*

FORMS OF THE PASSIVE VOICE

Tense	Active Voice		Passive Voice	
Simple present	offer,	offers	am, is, are	offered
Present progressive	am, is, are	offering	am, is, are	being offered
Simple past	offered		was, were	offered
Past progressive	was, were	offering	was, were	being offered
Future	shall, will	offer	shall, will	be offered
Present perfect	have, has	offered	have, has	been offered
Past perfect	had	offered	had	been offered
Future perfect	shall, will	have offered	shall, will	have been offered

The passive voice is preferred when the "doer" of an action (or, the agent) is unimportant or unknown. Because of its impersonal tone, the passive voice is commonly found in textbooks, in scientific, technical or business reports, and in newspaper stories.

---

[13]A **transitive** verb is a verb that *takes an object.*

Change the following sentences to passive form. Be sure to use the same tense as in the original sentence.

EXAMPLE: a. The janitor opens the door every morning.
The door is opened by the janitor every morning.
(Usually the **by**-phrase agent comes directly after the verb.)

b. Mr. Roberts will paint the murals in the new lecture hall.
The murals in the new lecture hall will be painted by Mr. Roberts.

c. His parents punished John for not going to school.
John was punished by his parents for not going to school.

d. The board has already discussed the matter.
The matter has already been discussed by the board.[14]

1. The court will try the case next week.

will be tried

2. His landlord asked him to move.

3. The heavy rains are ruining the crops.

The crops are being ruined by the heavy rains

4. A garage mechanic recognized the suspected killer.

The suspected killer was recognized by a garage mechanic.

5. Both houses of Congress have already passed the bill.

The bill has already been passed by both houses of Congress

6. The fire has entirely destroyed the house.

The house has entirely been destroyed by the fire

7. The store will deliver the furniture we ordered next week.

The furniture we ordered next week will be delivered (by the store)

8. All the students respect the new English teacher.

The new teacher is respected

9. His friends have recently given a party in his honor.

A party in his honor has recently been given

---

[14]Adverbs are placed after the first auxiliary. In a verb with two auxiliaries, only *-ly* adverbs of manner come after the second auxiliary.

[handwritten at top:]
The door is being closed
The door is closed
The door

10. The young couple had just bought the car when some teen-agers stole it. (*change both verbs*)

The car had just been bought (by the young couple when it was stolen (by some teen-ager.

11. The mechanic is repairing the refrigerator now.

The refrigerator is being repaired (by the mechanic).

12. A well-known art collector is donating several paintings to the museum. (*put **place** before the **by**-phrase agent*).

Several Paintings are being donated to the museum by a well-know art collector.

13. The contractors were still building the stadium when a strike halted all construction. (*change both verbs*)

The stadium was still being built (by the contra) when All Construction was halted (by a strike)

14. Their travel agent will have carefully planned their itinerary long before they start on their trip.

Their itinerary will have been carefully planned (by their Travel) long before they start on their trip.

15. A beautiful girl wearing a little white apron was serving the beverages.

The beverages were being served by a beautiful girl wearing a little white apron.

3-22
PASSIVE FORM OF VERBS (2)
— AGENT OMITTED

[handwritten:] The Person who is doing.

The agent is often omitted in passive sentences. In the following sentences containing passive verbs without agents, use the verb form required by the time expression.

EXAMPLE: a. The house (paint) every year.
The house is painted every year.

b. The proposal (consider) right now.
The proposal is being considered right now.

c. All the students' grades (distribute) next week.
All the students' grades will be distributed next week.

d. The matter (already, investigate).
The matter has already been investigated.

1. Much attention (devote) to this question at this time.

Much attention is being devoted to this question at this t.

2. The furniture (move) tomorrow.

will be moved

The furniture is being moved Tomorrow.

3. A new air conditioner (install) at this very moment.

A new air Conditioner is being installed

good — **4.** The merchandise (just, ship) when the order was canceled.

been

The merchandise had just shipped when we canceled

5. Their house (paint) when a fire broke out.

Their house was being Painted when a fire broke out

6. America (discover) in 1492.

America was discovered in 1492

7. Several of the culprits (already, punish).

Several of The culprits have already been Punished

8. He (know) throughout the world as a great scientist.

He is known Throughout the world as a great Scientist.

9. Most of the work (complete) before the strike began.

most of The work had been completed before the strike began.

10. Everything (already, do) to make the patient more comfortable.

Everything have already been done to make The Patient

11. All the food (eat) long before we get to the picnic.

All the food will be eaten long before we get to the Picinc.

12. Yesterday's parade (lead) by our high school band.

Yesterday's Parade was led by our high school band

13. The money which (donate) last week (soon, use) to buy food for the poor.

The money which was donated last week will soon be used to buy food for the Poor.

14. Her fur coat (just, take) out of storage when it was stolen.

Her fur coat had just been taken out of Storage when it was stolen

15. His political activities (investigate) by the government when he vanished from sight.

His Political activities were being investigated when he vanished from sight.

16. All the patients (evacuate) from the hospital by the time the enemy forces reach the area.

All the patients will be evacuated from the hospital by the Time the enemy forces reach the area.

3-23
PASSIVE OF VERBS
THAT TAKE TWO OBJECTS

With verbs that take indirect objects, either the direct or the indirect object may be the grammatical subject of the passive verb.

Active   The company will give us the guarantee in writing.

Passive   We will be given the guarantee in writing.
or
The guarantee will be given (to) us in writing.
(**To** is optional in the passive)

Give the two possible ways of restating the following sentences in the passive. Do not include the agent unless it is necessary for the meaning.

EXAMPLE: She sent her husband a telegram.
Her husband was sent a telegram.
A telegram was sent (to) her husband.

1. The company gave Mr. Jackson a notice of dismissal.

Mr. Jackson was given a notice of dismissal

A notice of dismissal was given to Mr. Jackson

2. We have mailed them the sample today.

They have been mailed the sample today.

The sample has been mailed to them today.

3. The waiter handed him the bill.

He was handed the bill.

The bill was handed to him.

4. The hotel is furnishing him everything he needs.

He is being furnished everything he needs.

Everything he needs is being furnished to him.

5. The child's aunt had brought him some warm clothes.

He had been brought some warm clothes.

Some warm clothes had been brought to him.

6. The teacher will teach the class the next lesson tomorrow.

The class will be taught the next lesson tomorrow.

The next lesson will be taught to the class tomorrow

7. An old resident had told us the whole story.

we had been Told The whole story (by an old resident)

The whole Story had been Told To us.

8. His employer had assigned him too many duties.

He had been assigned Too many duties.

Too many duties had been assigned To him.

9. The bank is lending him the money.

He is being lent The money (by The bank)

The money is being lent To him.

10. We won't refuse her this last request.

She wont be refused This last request.

This last request wont be refused To her.

11. The principal is writing her mother a letter now.

Her mother is being writen a letter now.

A letter is being writen To her mother now.

3-24
NEGATIVES OF VERBS

Verbs are made negative by adding **not** to them. The position of **not** depends on the number of auxiliaries with the verb.

Verbs with no auxiliaries (simple present and simple past tense only)					
be	Mary *is* late.	**Mary**	**is**	not		late.
all other verbs	Mary *arrived late.*	**Mary**	**did** (aux. added)	not	arrive	late.
Verbs with 1–3 auxiliaries					
1 aux	Mary *has arrived* late.	**Mary**	**has**	not	arrived	late.
2–3 aux.	Mary *has been arriving* late.	**Mary**	**has**	not	**been arriving**	late.

Negative contractions are made by combining an auxiliary (or a single form of **be, have**) with **not** and by using an apostrophe for the *o* that is omitted from **not**.

Examples: have + nøt = haven't

was + nøt = wasn't

do + nøt = don't

should + nøt = shouldn't

Some contractions are irregular:

$$can + n\emptyset t = can't$$
$$will + n\emptyset t = won't$$

There is a tendency to avoid the contractions **mayn't** and **mightn't**. **Shan't**, a contraction of **shall** and **not**, is not common in American usage.

Make the following sentences negative. Use contractions with **not**.

Verbs with No Auxiliaries

1. John is handsome.

_____

2. The boys are eager to go camping.

_____

3. It is very cold today.

_____

4. There is enough food for everyone.

_____

5. They were at home yesterday.

_____

6. She was curious about his being there.

_____

7. He drove to work today.

_____

8. She tells many lies.

_____

9. Some people like a warm climate.

_____

10. The police suspected him of stealing the money.

_____

11. They have a lot of money today.[15]

_____

[15] In negatives and questions, the simple present tense of **have** meaning *possess* may occur with or without the auxiliary **do**.

12. They had a lot of money last week.

_____

13. You ought to see him now.

_____

14. We have to make an immediate decision.

_____

15. They had to leave before the end of the meeting.

_____

Verbs with one Auxiliary

1. They are arriving next week.

_____

2. The students were behaving very badly.

_____

3. His money will last forever.

_____

4. He has found a suitable place to live.

_____

5. They have invited us to lunch.

_____

6. He can play tennis very well.

_____

7. We must close all the windows.

_____

8. The instruments have already arrived.[16]

_____

Verbs with Two to Three Auxiliaries

1. His political campaign is being financed by his friends.

_____

2. The doors will be opened before noon.

_____

[16]**Already** becomes **yet** in a negative; in a question **yet** is more common, but **already** is sometimes possible.

3. The money should be left in the cash register at night.

_____

4. The concert will have begun by 8 P.M.

_____

5. They might have moved from their old house.

_____

6. Car owners have been warned to lock their cars.

_____

3-25
YES-NO QUESTIONS

			Subject	Balance of predicate	
Verbs with no auxiliaries (simple present and simple past only)					
be	Mary *is* late.	**Is**	**Mary**		**late?**
all other verbs	Mary *arrived* late.	**Did** (aux. added.)	**Mary**	arrive	**late?**
Verbs with 1–3 auxiliaries					
1 aux.	Mary *has arrived* late.	**Has**	**Mary**	arrived	**late?**
2–3 aux.	Mary *has been arriving* late.	**Has**	**Mary**	been arriving	**late?**

Short answers to yes-no questions consist of: (1) a personal pronoun referring to the subject of the sentence, and (2) the verb form that starts the question.

Is Mary late?	Yes, she **is**.	or No, she **isn't**.
Did Mary arrive late?	Yes, she **did**.	or No, she **didn't**.
Has Mary arrived late?	Yes, she **has**.	or No, she **hasn't**.
Has Mary been arriving late?	Yes, she **has**.	or No, she **hasn't**.

Only **there** and impersonal **it** may also be used in a short answer to a **yes-no** question.

| Are **there** enough chairs? | Yes, **there** are. | or No, **there** aren't. |
| Is **it** raining? | Yes, **it** is. | or No, **it** isn't. |

In short answers, contractions are not made between the subject and the verb.

Change the sentences in Exercise 3-24 (pp. 73–75) to yes-no questions and give the short answers.

EXAMPLE: a. Is John handsome? Yes, he is. or No, he isn't.

  b. Are they arriving next week? Yes, they are. or No, they aren't.

Negative Yes-No Questions

Contractions with **not** are generally used in negative questions.

> **Isn't** Mary late?
> **Didn't** Mary **arrive** late?
> **Hasn't** Mary **arrived** late?
> **Hasn't** Mary **been arriving** late?

In more formal style without the contraction, **not** appears after the reversed verb-subject—**Is Mary not** late?

Change the sentences in Exercise 3-24 (pp. 73–75) to negative questions.

EXAMPLE: a. Isn't John handsome? _____

b. Aren't they arriving next week? _____

**Informal Omission
of Auxiliaries in Yes-No Questions**

In highly informal conversation, the initial auxiliary (or the independent verb **be**) and the subject **you** are sometimes omitted from a yes-no question.

Need any money?	for Do you need any money?
Found an apartment yet?	for Have you found an apartment yet?
Going with us tonight?	for Are you going with us tonight?

Supply the words that are "understood" in the following informal yes-no questions. Give short answers to these questions.

EXAMPLE: a. _____Do you_____ want to go to the movies?
Yes, I do, or No, I don't. _____

b. _____Have you_____ received the money yet?
Yes, I have, or No, I haven't. _____

c. _____Are you_____ excited about your trip?
Yes, I am, or No, I'm not. _____

1. _____ get the tickets?

_____

2. _____ ready to go soon?

_____

3. _____ drive to work today?

_____

4. _____ used to this climate yet?

_____

5. _____ told her the good news yet?

_____

6. _____ ever play tennis or badminton?

_____

7. _____ studying hard these days?

_____

8. _____ hear any more news about your scholarship?

_____

9. _____ had any luck lately at the horse races?

_____

10. _____ ever gone to the opera?

_____

11. _____ expecting someone?

_____

12. _____ ever find your wallet?

_____

3-26
QUESTIONS WITH INTERROGATIVE WORDS

Questions Beginning with Interrogative Adverbs— WHY? WHEN? WHERE? HOW?

Interrogative Adverb	Auxiliary (or *be*)	Subject	Balance of Predicate	
Why	*is*	Mary		late?
Why	*did* (aux. added)	Mary	arrive	late?
Why	*has*	Mary	arrived	late?
Why	*has*	Mary	been arriving	late?

How may combine with an adjective or adverb:

How tall are you?
How expensive is that dress?
How quickly can you get here?
How badly was he hurt?

What . . . for is an informal equivalent of **why**—*What* did you do that *for*?

Change the following sentences into as many questions as you can that begin with **when, where, why, how,** or **how** + an adjective or adverb.

EXAMPLE: a. Helen was in the main library for three hours.

Where was Helen for three hours?

How long was Helen in the library?

b. Marie has recently borrowed $1,000 to pay for her tuition.

When has Marie borrowed $1,000 to pay for her tuition?

Why has Marie borrowed $1,000?

c. The student from Japan is frequently absent because of illness.

Why is the student from Japan frequently absent?

How often is the student from Japan absent?

1. Luis is from Venezuela.

_____

_____

2. My friend goes to the theater once a week.

_____

_____

3. The Taylors returned the lawn mower to their neighbors right away.

_____

_____

4. Mr. Smith gave his wife a beautiful ring for her birthday.

_____

_____

5. Clara played tennis with Bob yesterday.

_____

_____

6. You ought to see a doctor if you have a fever.

_____

_____

7. Everyone at the meeting was asked to contribute money for the poor.

_____

_____

8. The maid has been cleaning the house thoroughly since yesterday.

_____

_____

9. Leo's employer is planning a big celebration in an expensive restaurant.

_____

_____

10. The girl is taking her younger brother to the movies.

_____

_____

11. The front door should be carefully locked when you leave the house.

_____

_____

12. She went to the bakery for bread. (*include* **what . . . for**)

_____

_____

13. All the volunteers for evening work must report to the office immediately.

_____

_____

14. Mrs. Jones asked her husband for more money.

_____

_____

15. His wife's new coat cost $150.

_____

_____

16. Mr. Anderson will put half of his salary in the bank today.

_____

_____

17. Mr. Brown's secretary went to the post office to get some stamps. (*include* **what . . . for**)

_____

_____

18. George will travel to the West Coast by bus.

_____

_____

19. She can type fifty words a minute.

_____

_____

20. Their son is five years old.

_____

_____

21. His uncle sends him an expensive gift every year.

_____

_____

22. The doctor left his car at the service station because it needed a new battery.

_____

_____

Questions Beginning with Interrogative Pronouns

1. **Who** (**whom** for object, **whose** for possessive)—for persons
2. **What**—for things
3. **Which**—for persons or things, when a choice is involved

Interrogative pronoun as:				
object of verb	**Whom**	**do**	**you**	**want?** (*informal*—Who do you want?)
	What	**can**	**I**	**do for you?**
object of preposition	**To whom**	**is**	**he**	**speaking?** (*informal*—Who(m) is he speaking to?)
	On what	**will**	**he**	**lecture?** (*informal*—What will he lecture on?)
subject of verb			**Who**	**invented the telephone?**
			What	**has caused the accident?**

Change the sentences on pp. 78–80 into as many questions as you can using the interrogative pronouns **who** (or **whom, whose**) **what, which.**

EXAMPLE: a. Who was in the main library for three hours?

b. Who has recently borrowed $100 to pay for her tuition?
   What has Marie recently borrowed to pay for her tuition?

c. Who is frequently absent because of illness?

3-27
QUESTIONS WITH
INTERROGATIVE ADJECTIVES
WHOSE, WHAT, WHICH

Interrogative adjective with:	
subject	**What** guarantee comes with this television set? **Which** bus goes to Main Street?
object	**What** guarantee can you give? **Which** bus shall I take?
object of preposition	From **whose** garden did you get these flowers? To **which** post office should this be taken? On **what** grounds are you suing him?

Based on the italicized phrases, form questions using **whose, what, which** as interrogative adjectives. Keep in mind that **which** implies a choice (of persons or of things), **what** merely elicits information.

EXAMPLE: a. He is taking *the 10: 30 bus.*
Which bus is he taking?

b. He is taking a vacation *on his doctor's advice.*
On whose advice is he taking a vacation?

c. He is arriving *at 5 o'clock.*
At what time is he arriving? (**At** may be omitted.)

1. *Mr. Smith's store* is going to be sold.

2. They live *on 72nd Street.*

3. They sat *in the last row.*

4. They are going to transplant *the tree on the front lawn.*

5. *His father's friend* scolded him.

6. *All the students* were punished.

7. *Pan-American Airlines* has a flight at that time.

8. She's wearing *her sister's sweater*.

---

9. They canceled the play *because the star became ill*. (Use **for what reason**.)

3-28
ATTACHED QUESTIONS

This kind of yes-no question consists of two parts. The first part makes a *statement*; the second part asks the question that expects agreement with the statement. The second part contains the regular question auxiliary plus the personal pronoun that stands for the subject (or the expletives **it**, **there**).

Question		*Expected Answer*
Mary **is** late,	**is'nt** she?	Yes, she is.
Mary **isn't** late,	**is** she?	No, she isn't.
Mary **arrived** late,	**didn't** she?	Yes, she did.
Mary **didn't** arrive late,	**did** she?	No, she didn't.
Mary **has** arrived late,	**hasn't** she?	Yes, she has.
Mary **hasn't** arrived late,	**has** she?	No, she hasn't.
Mary **has** been arriving late,	**hasn't** she?	Yes, she has.
Mary **hasn't** been arriving late,	**has** she?	No, she hasn't.

Note that the attached part of the question begins with the same auxiliary (or the independent verb **be**) as the simple yes-no question. Note also that each question contains a positive-negative or a negative-positive contrast.

Change the following statements into attached questions expecting (1) the answer *yes*, (2) the answer *no.* Give the expected short answers.

EXAMPLE: a. The girl remembers you.

The girl remembers you, doesn't she? Yes, she does.

The girl doesn't remember you, does she? No, she doesn't.

b. There is a piano in the room.

There is a piano in the room, isn't there? Yes, there is.

There isn't a piano in the room, is there? No, there isn't.

1. Mr. Brown is rich.

---

2. Janice broke her arm.

_____

_____

3. The coffee will be ready soon.

_____

_____

4. He has been having financial trouble.

_____

_____

5. The post office is far from here.

_____

_____

6. It is cold outside.

_____

_____

7. You take cream with your coffee.

_____

_____

8. The plane will be landing soon.

_____

_____

9. The reservations have already been made.

_____

_____

10. The janitor shut the door.

_____

_____

11. The old house burned down.

_____

_____

12. It's hard to do that.

_____

_____

13. There were many people in the room.

_____

_____

14. The calendars have been ordered.

_____

_____

15. He can come with us.

_____

_____

16. They could have left the office early.[17]

_____

_____

17. There is someone at the door.[18]

_____

_____

18. It is beginning to snow.

_____

_____

19. The police caught the thief.

_____

_____

[17]Sometimes **have** as a second auxiliary is included in a short answer—**Yes, they could have.**
[18]**Some** becomes **any** in the negative.

4

Auxiliaries

TYPES OF AUXILIARIES

Tense	be	+	-ing present participle for *progressive* forms	He *is opening* the door now.
	be	+	-ed past participle for *passive* forms	Many soldiers *were wounded* in the battle.
	have	+	-ed past participle for the *perfect* tenses	They *have* just *arrived*.
	shall—will	+	simple form of verb for the *future* tense	They *will arrive* soon.
Questions, negatives of auxiliary-less verbs	do	+	simple form of verb	*Did* he *arrive* on time? He *didn't arrive* on time.
Modal	**can—could** **may—might** **should** **would** **must** **be able to**[1] **ought to**[1] **have to**[1]		} + simple form of verb	He *can* *should* } speak English. *must*
	These modal auxiliaries add a special meaning such as *ability, permission, possibility*, etc., to the meaning of the main part of the verb.			

The first exercises in this chapter will be concerned with the forms of verb phrases containing auxiliaries; the next exercises will concentrate mainly on the special meanings of the modal auxiliaries.

[1] It is customary to include these verbs followed by **to** among the modals not only because they are semantic equivalents of the modals listed here but also because they form negatives and questions in the same way as modal auxiliaries do.

VERB FORMS WITH ONE AUXILIARY

am is are was were	**offering** (progressive) *or* **offered** (passive)	have has had	**offered** (perfect)	do shall—should will—would can—could may—might must	**offer**

Use the correct form of the verb.

EXAMPLE: a. They are (open) _____ opening _____ the store right now.

b. All these houses were (sell) _____ sold _____ last year.

c. We have finally (finish) _____ finished _____ the work.

d. We can (be) _____ be _____ there at five o'clock.

1. The windows were (clean) _____ yesterday.

2. She is (study) _____ very hard this year.

3. She has (choose) _____ a fine profession.

4. He should (arrive) _____ in a few hours.

5. They were (argue) _____ bitterly when I met them.

6. He has (mislay) _____ the money somewhere.

7. They might (visit) _____ us tomorrow.

8. The hunter was (attack) _____ by a bear.

9. I would (appreciate) _____ it if you would keep quiet.

10. The bills were (pay) _____ last week.

11. She has (bring) _____ her children with her.

12. The two men were already (fight) _____ when the police came.

13. The thief was (catch) _____ a few hours ago.

14. Her jewelry is (keep) _____ in a locked drawer.

15. Are the books still (lie) _____ on the table?

16. Have they (dig) _____ the foundation yet?

17. Were they (permit) _____ to leave the country?

18. Shall I (serve) _____ the dinner now?[2]

---

[2] **Shall** used in this kind of question is the equivalent of **Do you want me to, Would you like me to?**

VERB FORMS WITH TWO AUXILIARIES (1)
BE, BEEN AS THE SECOND AUXILIARY

Active Progressive (With *-ING* Participle)

Present Form of First Auxiliary	*Past Form of First Auxiliary*
have has } **been offering**	had **been offering**
will shall can may must } **be offering**	would should could might } **be offering**

Use the correct form of the **progressive**.

EXAMPLE: a. They (will leave) _____ be leaving _____ for London tomorrow.
       b. Guests (have come) _____ have been coming _____ in and out all day today.
       c. (He has lived) _____ Has he been living _____ in the same house all his life?

1. I (shall stay) _____ at my friends' house next week.

2. You (can do) _____ your homework while I get dinner ready.

3. I don't know where my husband is; he (may visit) _____ one of our neighbors.

4. My secretary isn't at her desk; she (must take) _____ her afternoon break.

5. They told us that they (had waited) _____ for more than two hours.

6. He (would go) _____ to the university now if his father hadn't lost his money in the stock market.

7. The play (should end) _____ soon; it's almost 11:00 P.M.

8. The enemy (could prepare) _____ for a new attack; intelligence sources report that increased supplies are being brought in.

9. Let's take an umbrella; it (might rain) _____ when we get out of the theater.

10. He (will come) _____ in on the six o'clock train.

11. (He has caused) _____ any more disturbances in school?

12. (The plants should get) _____ more water?

Passive (With *-ED* Participle)
(*BE, BEING, BEEN* as the Second Auxiliary)

Present Form of First Auxiliary		Past Form of First Auxiliary	
have has }	**been offered**	had **been offered**	
am is are }	**being offered**	was were }	**being offered**
will shall can may must }	**be offered**	would should could might }	**be offered**

Use the correct form of the **passive voice**.

EXAMPLE: a. The troops (have instructed) _____*have been instructed*_____ to get ready to leave at once.
   b. The doors (will open) _____*will be opened*_____ at 10:00 A.M.
   c. (He might stop) _____*Might he be stopped*_____ if he tries to cross the border?

1. We (shall sue) _____ by the landlord if we don't pay the back rent at once.

2. The job (can finish) _____ on time if all the employees work overtime for a few days.

3. All traffic violators (shall fine)[3] _____ heavily.

4. All parcels (must wrap) _____ so that they (may open) _____ for postal inspection.

5. The children (be served) _____ dinner when some of their friends came to see them.

6. He (had just made) _____ a partner in his law firm when he suffered a severe heart attack.

7. If the boy returned to his family, he (would forgive) _____ for running away.

8. The superintendent of the building (should notify) _____ in case of any emergency.

9. If he were here now, that problem (could solve) _____ easily.

10. If he (had offered) _____ a gift, he would have refused it.

11. The books which (must read) _____ by the students in the class (have listed) _____ on the sheet which (be handed out) _____ now.

12. (He should allow) _____ to do whatever he pleases?

13. These items (are put) _____ on sale tomorrow.

[3]**Shall** used with the third person often represents legal or commercial usage.

14. This letter (must retype) _____ ; there are too many errors in it.

15. (They, will offend) _____ if we don't come to their party?

16. (The office, have notified) _____ of his illness?

4-3
VERB FORMS WITH TWO AUXILIARIES (2)
HAVE AS THE SECOND AUXILIARY

Active Voice (With -ED Participle)

Present Form of First Auxiliary	*Past Form of First Auxiliary*
will shall can[4] may must } **have offered**	would should could might } **have offered**

Use the correct form of the verb with **have as the second auxiliary**.

EXAMPLE: a. They (will leave) _____ will have left _____ the city long before we get there.

      b. She (must be) _____ must have been _____ in a great hurry to leave for the theater because she left all the dinner dishes on the table.

      c. (The accident might occur) __ Might the accident have occurred __ as he described it?

1. That store has just gone bankrupt. I believe they (should have) _____ _____ a stricter policy about giving people credit.

2. That store (might not go) _____ bankrupt if they had had a stricter policy about giving people credit.

3. I can't find my keys; I (may leave) _____ them at home.

4. We (would meet) _____ you at the station if we had known you were coming.

5. The plants (must die) _____ because no one watered them.

6. Next week, the painters (will be) _____ on strike for half a year.

7. They (must lose) _____ a great deal of money in the stock market.

8. He (would win) _____ the tennis match if he had not sprained his ankle.

9. If you had done those exercises, you (might benefit) _____ from them.

10. He (might plan) _____ the whole thing himself.

11. We (shall travel) _____ a thousand miles by the end of the month.

[4]**Can have offered** is not commonly used.

12. Many children (will die) _____ before the war is over.

13. If he had wanted to, (he could send) _____ the money?

14. (The forest fire could start) _____ from a campfire that was not carefully put out?

4-4

VERB FORMS WITH THREE AUXILIARIES
HAVE AS THE SECOND AUXILIARY

Active Progressive (With -ING Participle)

Present Form of First Auxiliary		*Past Form of First Auxiliary*	
will shall can[5] may must	**have been offering**	would should could might	**have been offering**

Use the correct form of the **progressive** with *have* as the second auxiliary.

EXAMPLE: He (may steal) _____ may have been stealing _____ for a long time without his parents knowing about it.

1. He (must sleep) _____ so soundly that he didn't hear the alarm go off.

2. They (will rehearse) _____ for an hour by the time we get there.

3. On November 20, I (shall do) _____ the same work for thirty years.

4. The girl (may smoke) _____ for some time before her mother caught her doing it.

5. We're sorry our plane is so late in arriving. You (must wait) _____ a long time.

6. You (should do) _____ your homework last night instead of watching television.

7. You (would live) _____ in luxury for some time if you had taken your stockbroker's advice.

8. Those men (must smuggle) _____ in the jewelry for several years before they were caught.

9. He (should save) _____ for the future instead of spending all his money on luxuries.

10. He (could not work) _____ at that time, because he was just recovering from a serious operation.

[5]**Can have been offering** is not commonly used.

11. Only those personnel that had access to the telegraph (could send) _____ _____ the messages to the enemy.

12. He (must do) _____ extremely well in his schoolwork, because he was offered scholarships from several fine universities.

13. The thieves (must watch) _____ the house for some time before they broke into it.

Passive Voice (With -ED Participle)

Present Form of First Auxiliary		Past Form of First Auxiliary	
will shall can[6] may must	**have been offered**	would should could might	**have been offered**

Use the correct form of the **passive** with *have* as the second auxiliary.

EXAMPLE: a. For all we know, the child (may abandon) ___may have been abandoned___ by its mother some time ago.

b. The money (would send) ___would have been sent___ to you at once if we had known your address.

c. (The fire might start) ___Might the fire have been started___ by an arsonist?

1. Surely the package (will receive) _____ by now.

2. The door (must leave) _____ open, because the thief seems to have entered the house without any difficulty.

3. They (should inform) _____ by the company that their insurance was about to expire.

4. The automobile accident (could prevent) _____ if he had been more alert.

5. The gangster (might shoot) _____ by a rival gangster.

6. Thousands of people (must kill) _____ by the eruptions of Mt. Vesuvius.

7. The bill (would veto) _____ by the President if certain changes had not been made in it.

8. The rehearsal (must cancel) _____ because the theater is dark.

9. He (should allow) _____ to say a few words in his defense.

10. The car (should not drive) _____ so fast in that heavy traffic.

11. The burning building (may strike) _____ by lightning.

[6] **Can have been offered** is not commonly used.

12. (The letter might write) _____ by the
mayor himself?

13. (The injured man could strike) _____
by a heavy object?

4-5
ABILITY

CAN (PAST *COULD*), *BE ABLE TO* (ALL TENSES)

Physical ability	I can (*or* am able to) lift this stone.
Learned ability	She can (*or* is able to) type.
Have the power to	I can see you tonight.
	This factory can produce dozens of machines a day.

It is only in this third sense of ability (which is related to possibility), that **can**
and, to a lesser extent **be able to**, may refer to future time. **Be able to** is generally not
used with a passive verb.

Use the correct form of **can** and **be able to** (where possible).

EXAMPLE: a. When I was a boy, I (speak) __could speak *or* was able to speak__ several foreign languages,
but now I (speak) __can speak *or* am able to speak__ only one foreign language.
b. This error (correct) _____ can be corrected _____ easily.

1. No one (go) _____ without sleep indefinitely.

2. (You reach) _____ the top shelf of the cabinet?

3. She (swim) _____ several miles without getting tired.

4. He (not paint) _____ the whole house in one day.

5. This kind of dress (make) _____ with very little material.

6. The bank repossessed his car because he (not keep up) _____
_____ his payments.

7. (you have) _____ dinner with me tonight?

8. She loves chocolates. She (eat) _____ a whole box herself.

9. The car ran out of gas, so they (not go) _____ any farther.

10. Why (you, not lend) _____ him some money last week?

11. John thought he (pass) _____ the examination.

12. That matter (settle) _____ only by heads of state.

13. (The typist, finish) _____ all the letters today?

14. The error (correct) _____ very easily.

15. He said that he (move) _____ the piano without any help.

16. My watch is very old; it (not repair) _____ any more.

4-6
PERMISSION
MAY (PAST *MIGHT*), *CAN* (PAST *COULD*)

	Question (requesting permission)	Permission being granted
First person	May (*or* can) I borrow your car?	You may (*or* can) borrow my car if you drive carefully.
Third person	May (*or* can) John come to the movies with us?	Yes, John may go to the movies with you.

Can used for permission is considered informal. The past forms of **may** and **can** are also used in requests—**Might** (or **could**) **I borrow your car?**[7]

May or **can** are also used in the sense of *be permitted*. In this sense, the past forms **might** and **could** express only past time.

Present or "timeless" time	Anyone may (*or* can) enroll for this course.
Past time	In those days, anyone might (*or* could) enroll for the course.

In the sequence of tenses **might** and **could** also indicate only past time.

Present time	John's mother **says** that he **may** (*or* can) go with us.
Past time	John's mother **said** that he **might** (*or* could) go with us.

Use the correct form of **may** or **can**.

EXAMPLE: a. (I see) _____ May I see *or* Can I see _____ you tonight?
       b. (I permit) _____ May I be permitted _____ to look for the book myself?

1. (I come) _____ in?

2. (I help) _____ you carry those packages?

3. (I leave) _____ the office a little early today?

4. (The children come over) _____ to play with my children?

5. Yes, they _____, if they are back by dinner time.

6. Anyone (attend) _____ our church services.

7. Our teacher told us we (take) _____ one hour off to do some research in the library.

8. Students (attend) _____ the performance free if they get their tickets in advance.

[7]Where there is a choice between a present or past modal, the past form usually lessens the force of the modal.

9. Anyone who has a library card (take out) _____ books from the library.

10. (I be excused) _____ from class early today?

11. Until recently, anyone (enter) _____ the factory without permission.

4-7

OBLIGATION, ADVISABILITY
SHOULD, OUGHT TO, HAD BETTER

Should, ought to, had better occur in statements about one's duty or advantage which one is free to accept or reject.

1. *Obligation* (What one is expected to do)—**You should** (*or* **ought to**) **do your homework every day.**
2. *Advisability* (What is wise for one to do)—**She should** (*or* **ought to**, *or* **had better**) **eat less if she wants to lose weight.**

The forms used for past time, **should have, ought to have,** imply that the action was not performed. **Had better** has no past form.

Use both **should** and **ought to** where possible. Use the correct form of the auxiliary.

EXAMPLE: a. Everyone (go) _____should go, (*or* ought to go)_____ to the dentist once a year.
b. Mr. Johnson (go) _should have gone (*or* ought to have gone)_ to the dentist yesterday, but he was too busy. (Mr. Johnson didn't go to the dentist.)

1. You (help) _____ your mother with the housework.

2. He (give) _____ his wife more money than he does.

3. The airconditioner (clean) _____ once a year.

4. There was a question of whether he (allow) _____ to hold two jobs at once.

5. I (write) _____ some letters tonight, but I have a headache.

6. Everyone (save) _____ for a rainy day.

7. We (not leave) _____ the door unlocked when we left the house.

8. The boys (punish) _____ yesterday because of the damage they caused.

9. I (study—*progressive*) _____ for my examination now instead of reading the comics.

10. Why (I not have) _____ the same rights as you?

11. Why (they punish) _____ the boy so severely yesterday?

12. I (look) _____ into this matter a long time ago.

13. His friends (help) _____ him when he was in trouble instead of criticizing him.

14. We (take) _____ more precautions against fire; if we had we would still have our house.

15. I think you (see) _____ Mr. Jones about that matter now.

16. Henry (study) _____ last night, but he went to the movies instead.

17. My physician told me I (make) _____ an appointment soon.

18. Traffic laws (obey) _____ by motorists and pedestrians.

Based on the sentence given below, tell what someone *had better do.*

EXAMPLE: a. Jack has a bad cold.
He'd better stay in bed.

b. It's raining very hard outside.
We'd better not go to the movies.

1. This melon isn't ripe yet.

2. The phone is ringing.

3. His shoes are worn out.

4. Mary spilled some coffee on her dress.

5. The point of this pencil isn't sharp any more.

6. We've done enough work today.

7. Lucy has a bad toothache.

8. We've been driving all day.

9. There's a storm approaching.

10. We're running out of gas.

4-8
POSSIBILITY
MAY, CAN

May is the usual auxiliary for possibility.

Present or future time	It may (*or* might) rain tonight. (*Might* expresses less certainty.)
Past time	He may (*or* might) have gone to the party last night.

Can is also common as an auxiliary expressing possibility. This use is related to ability when the subject refers to a person.

Present or future time	Something can (*or* may) go wrong. *or* Something could (*or* might) go wrong.
Past time	Something could (*or* may, might) have gone wrong.

Note that **may have**, **might have**, **could have** are used only for *past possibility*, not for permission or ability.

Use the correct form of **may** or **can** for possibility. In some sentences only **may** expresses possibility.

EXAMPLE: a. It looks as though it (snow) _____ may (*or* might) snow _____ soon.
b. I can't find my umbrella. I (leave) ____ may (*or* might, could) have left ____ it at the office.
c. If the heavy rains continue, they (damage) __ may (*or* might, can, could) damage __ the crops.
d. They (try) ____ might (*or* could) be trying ____ to phone us right now.
e. He (pass) ____ might (*or* could) have passed ____ the examination if he had studied harder.
f. (The missing child, kidnap) __ could (*or* might) the missing child have been kidnaped __ yesterday?

1. You (be) _____ right after all.

2. The jury (decide) _____ that he is really innocent even though there is much circumstantial evidence against him.

3. These products (purchase) _____ at any drug store.

4. What (cause) _____ the delay now?

5. (He be) _____ at his home rather than at his office at this hour?

6. His plane (shoot down) _____ on his last flight over enemy territory.

7. They (have) _____ dinner right now.

8. John said he (be able) _____ to go on the trip, but he wasn't sure.

9. He (cheat) _____ at cards when he was shot by one of the players.

10. What would you do if you (do) _____ anything you wanted to?

11. You (interest) _____ in looking over this travel folder.

12. He (look, *progressive*) _____ for an excuse not to do the job.

13. She (not be) _____ able to find her husband in that crowd.[8]

14. When they return to their home town, they (not find) _____ _____ anyone they know.

15. We (not come) _____ if we had known you would not be there.

4-9
NECESSITY
MUST, HAVE TO

The difference between obligation and necessity is often one of degree only. While statements with **should** and **ought to** suggest a desirable course of action, statements with **must** and **have to** suggest a more urgent course of action. **Must** is generally felt as stronger than **have to**.

In the sense of necessity, the past form for **must** is **had to**—**I had to meet my cousin yesterday.** This past form is required in the sequence of tenses. Thus, **He *tells* me I *must* do it** becomes **He told me I *had to* do it.**[9]

Have got to is an informal equivalent of **have to**. It has only a present form.

Use the correct form of **must** or **have to**. Use both auxiliaries if they are possible.

EXAMPLE: a. I (leave) ____must leave *or* have to leave____ right away.
         b. I (leave) _____had to leave_____ the party early last night.
         c. You (not sit) _____mustn't sit_____ so close to the fire. (**Must not** is used for a prohibition or a warning.)
         d. You (not pay) _____don't have to pay_____ in person; you can pay by check. (**not have to** = not be required to)
         e. (We write) Must we write *or* Do we have to write a thesis in order to get a degree? (Only the **do** auxiliary is used in questions and negatives with **have to**.)

1. I (go) _____ to the bank to make a deposit.

2. You (pay) _____ your rent at once or I will have you evicted.

3. We (eat) _____ in order to live.

4. He asked the teacher whether he (hand in) _____ his composition immediately even though he hadn't finished it.

5. He feels he (read) _____ every book on the subject before he can write his own book.

6. (You make) _____ so much noise?

[8]Usually only **may** (or **might**) is used for negative possibility.
[9]In informal English, the present form **must** is often heard in sequence of tenses—**He told me I must do it.**

7. Students (not write) _____ their homework in pencil.

8. You (not go) _____ home if you don't want to. You can stay here overnight.

9. I have often wondered whether he (do) _____ what he did.

10. They (sell) _____ their home in order to pay off all their debts.

11. You (not copy) _____ from others during an examination.

12. They (comply) _____ with the building code, or they will not be granted permission to build.[10]

13. Students (not attend) _____ classes on Fridays.

14. All books (return) _____ by the end of the term.

15. Years ago people (read) _____ by candlelight.

16. (Everyone go) _____ to the meeting tomorrow?

17. We (not be) _____ late for the meeting.

18. Students (attend) _____ all classes. However, they (not participate) _____ in extracurricular activities.

19. You (not touch) _____ that wire or you'll get an electric shock.

20. (You leave) _____ so early?

4-10
INFERENCE WITH *MUST*

Must is often used to make a guess about an event in the present or in the past.

I hear the sound of fire engines. **There must be a fire nearby.** (Inference about the present.)
Yesterday I went to a music festival. **There must have been 1,000 people in the audience.** (Inference about past time. **Must have** is used only for past inference, not past necessity.)

Tell what can be inferred from the following statements. Possibilities are suggested by the words in parentheses.

Inference About Present Time

EXAMPLE: a. I haven't seen her for a few days. (sick)
   She must be sick.

   b. There is a big furniture van in front of our neighbors' house. (moving)
   They must be moving.

   c. The boys are carrying sleeping bags. (go on a camping trip)
   They must be going on a camping trip.

1. The cat has not been eating all day. (not feel well)

[10]**Will** may be used with **have to.**

2. Look out the window. There's almost no one out in the street today. (very cold)

_____

3. This milk is very thin and watery. (skim milk)

_____

4. The students entering the classroom are carrying wet umbrellas. (rain)

_____

5. He owns a boat and an airplane. (very rich)

_____

6. The grandstand benches are being put out on the street. (get ready for a big parade)

_____

7. Nobody answers the phone. (out to lunch)

_____

8. The dentist will not take any new patients now. (very busy)

_____

9. The door won't open. (not have the right key)

_____

10. He was too busy to eat lunch. (very hungry now)

_____

11. I've tried to call them several times today. (not be in town)

_____

Inference About Past Time

EXAMPLE:　a.　I can't find my watch anywhere. (lose)
　　　　　　　I must have lost it.
_____

　　　　　　b.　The coffee tastes bitter. (boil too long)
　　　　　　　It must have been boiling too long.
_____

1. I never received your letter. (lose in the mails)

_____

2. When he walked into the classroom the students were busy writing. (take a test)

_____

3. The ground is covered with snow. (snow last night)

_____

4. The cake is burned on the edges. (be in the oven too long)

_____

5. Her hair looks beautiful today. (go to the hairdresser's)

_____

6. The children returned from the picnic tired but in good spirits. (have a good time)

_____

7. Look at this picture of my grandmother. (be very beautiful when she was young)

_____

8. The plane hasn't arrived yet. (delay because of the bad weather)

_____

9. I can't find my wallet. (leave at home)

_____

10. There's a mistake in my figures. (not add right)

_____

4-11
EXPECTATION, *SHOULD*

In addition to obligation or advisability, **should**—and to a lesser extent **ought to** —may indicate expectation.

Present or future	It's five o'clock. The train should (*or* ought to) be here any moment.
Past	I sent the package a week ago It should (*or* ought to) have arrived by now. I don't know what's the matter. The train should have been here an hour ago. (*expectation not realized*)

A. In the following sentence, use **should** for expectation with reference to the present, or **should have** with reference to the past.

EXAMPLE: a. I _____ should _____ finish this letter by 10 o'clock.
   b. We ordered the books months ago. They (arrive) ____ should have arrived ____ long before now.

1. The messenger is on his way. He (get) _____ to your office in a few minutes.

2. He (be back) _____ from his hunting trip any day now.

3. The doctor thinks he (get—*progressive*) _____ better soon.

4. We don't understand what's delaying them. They (be) _____ here an hour ago.

5. Mr. Harris is busy now, but he (be) _____ able to see you in a few minutes.

6. My wife is preparing dinner now. It (be) _____ ready soon.

7. People are getting on the bus now. It (leave—*progressive*) _____ _____ in a few minutes.

8. I'm beginning to get worried. They (write) _____ us long before this.

9. It's a clear day. The stars (be) _____ very bright tonight.

10. Look in that cabinet. The files you want (be) _____ there.

11. The plane is just now landing. It (arrive) _____ hours ago.

12. The snow has stopped falling. We (be) _____ able to go out soon.

B. Go over the sentences in A using **ought to, ought to have** instead of **should, should have.**

EXAMPLE: a. I ought to finish this letter by 10 o'clock. _____

             b. We ordered the books months ago. They ought to have arrived long before now. _____

Should for expectation is related to **must** for inference. Occasionally these auxiliaries are interchangeable, **must** merely expressing a greater degree of certainty.

We airmailed the letter a few days ago. It should (or must) be there now.
We airmailed the letter a few days ago. It should have (or must have) arrived by now.

However, while **should** may be used for future expectation (**It should arrive soon**), **must** cannot be used for future inference.

Use **should** or **should have** for expectation, or **must** or **must have** for inference. In some sentences, two choices are possible.

EXAMPLE: a. I don't see him anywhere. He (be) _____ must be _____ out to lunch.
             b. The cake has been in the oven for 35 minutes. It (be) _____ should *or* must be _____ ready.
             c. His credit card was mailed a week ago. He (receive) _____ should *or* must have received _____ it by now.
             d. One of my classmates looks quite depressed. He (not pass) _____ must not have _____ passed _____ the examination.

1. His temperature is going down. He (feel) _____ better soon.

2. I can't find my umbrella. I (leave) _____ it at the office.

3. What's keeping him? He (be) _____ here a long time ago.

4. The plane has been missing for a week. It (crash) _____ in the mountains during the storm.

5. The trip from the airport takes only half an hour. He (be) _____ _____ here an hour ago.

6. He has extended his visit to Hawaii. He (enjoy—*progressive*) _____ _____ the balmy breezes there.

7. The check has just been sent out. You (get) _____ it in a day or two.

8. They have never acknowledged receipt of my gift. They (not receive) _____ _____ it.

9. The girl didn't answer when the teacher called on her. She (be) _____ _____ daydreaming.

10. There's no heat today. Something (go) _____ wrong with the furnace.

11. Something is wrong. The heat (come up) _____ an hour ago.

12. I can't get a dial tone on this telephone. It (be) _____ out of order.

13. He is smoking a strong cigar. He (not be) _____ aware that it is disturbing some of the guests.

14. The lunar spaceship is already in orbit around the earth. It (reach) _____ _____ the moon in a few days.

15. I've just turned on the air conditioner. It (start) _____ to get cool here soon.

16. She's still working at her desk. She (not realize) _____ that it's time to leave.

17. She's typing the last page. It (not take) _____ her much longer to finish the letter.

18. It's 7:30. The play (start—*progressive*) _____ soon.

4-12
WOULD RATHER

Would rather[11], which is a synonym for *prefer*, is often included among the auxiliaries. It may refer to present or past time.

Present (*now, or in general*)	I **would rather wear** a fur coat than a cloth coat in the winter.
Past	I **would rather have worn** a fur coat than a cloth coat last winter.

---

[11]**Had rather** is an older variant of **would rather**.

A. Replace the sentences with **prefer** with sentences containing **would rather** plus the words in parentheses. (Write your answers on the lines marked A.)

EXAMPLE: a. She prefers   dancing   to   anything else.
                    (go dancing)   (do anything else)
    A. <u>She would rather go dancing than do anything else.</u>
    b. The Browns prefer   the movies   to   the theater.
                    (go to the movies)   (go to the theater)
    A. <u>The Browns would rather go to the movies than (go) to the theater.</u>
    (If the second verb is the same as the first, it is often omitted.)

1. We all prefer   peace   to   war.
                    (have peace)   (be at war)

    A. _____

    B. _____

2. Mrs. Jones prefers   France   to   England.
                    (live in France)   (live in England)

    A. _____

    B. _____

3. The children prefer   the porch   to   the bedroom.
                    (sleep in the porch)   (sleep in the bedroom)

    A. _____

    B. _____

4. He prefers   the ocean   to   a lake.
                    (swim in the ocean)   (swim in a lake)

    A. _____

    B. _____

5. They prefer staying at home to going out on New Year's Eve.
                    (stay at home)   (go out on New Year's Eve)

    A. _____

    B. _____

6. They prefer eating at home to eating in a restaurant.
                    (eat at home)   (eat in a restaurant)

    A. _____

    B. _____

B. Change the sentences in A using **would rather have** to express *past preference.* (Write your answers on the lines marked B.)

EXAMPLE: a. B. <u>She would rather have gone dancing than (have) done anything else.</u>
       b. B. <u>The Browns would rather have gone to the movies than (have gone) to the theater.</u>

C. **Would rather** is sometimes confused with **had better**. What must be kept in mind is that **would rather** has the meaning of *preference,* and **had better** signifies *advisability.*

It's getting late. We'd better leave the office now or we'll miss the last bus.
   (we'd better = it would be advisable for us to)
I'd rather take a taxi home than ruin my clothes in the rain. (I'd rather = I would prefer to)

Use **had better, would rather, would rather have.**

EXAMPLE: a. He (paint) _____would rather paint_____ than do anything else.
   b. In the past, the elderly couple (travel) _____would rather have traveled_____ than stayed at home.
   c. I think we (not take) _____had better not take_____ a vacation this year.

1. I (be) _____ right than President.

2. Adam and Eve (stay) _____ in the Garden of Eden than been expelled from it.

3. He told the police that he (go) _____ to prison than betray his friend.

4. The doctor told her she (sleep) _____ on a hard mattress if she wanted to avoid backaches.

5. In the last war, the young children (go) _____ to school than sought shelter from bombs.

6. We (take) _____ the clothes off the line before it starts to rain.

7. He (eat) _____ more sensibly if he doesn't want to get sick.

8. He (commute) _____ from the suburbs than live in the city.

9. I (do) _____ things for myself than ask other people to do them for me.

10. You (not waste) _____ so much time if you want to catch the train.

11. When he was a child, he (have) _____ love than material things.

12. I think you (see) _____ the doctor right away.

13. If I have a choice, I (not continue) _____ my studies at this school.

14. The hotel clerk asked the guests whether they (have) _____ a room facing the mountains or the sea.

15. The children were told that they (not feed) _____ the animals in the zoo.

16. I (go) _____ to Europe by boat than by plane.

4-13
AUXILIARIES WITH *TO*

The modal auxiliaries with **to** that have already been given are **be able to** (= **can**), **ought to** (= **should**), and **have to** or informal **have got to** (= **must**). Other auxiliaries with **to** are:

1. **Used to**—meaning past custom[12]

> He *used to play* tennis very often when he was young.
>
> negative—He *didn't use to play* tennis very often when he was young.
>
> question—*Did he use to play* tennis very often when he was young?

Other ways of expressing past custom are with the auxiliary **would** or with the simple past—**He would play** (or **played**) **tennis very often when he was young.**

2. **Be to**—meaning be required to, be supposed to, be scheduled to

> You were to do your homework in ink.
>
> The train is to leave late tonight.

In the following sentences, change the auxiliaries to the synonomous forms with **to** (**be able to, ought to, have to** or informal **have got to**). Also, change **be required to, be supposed to, be scheduled to** to **be to**.

EXAMPLE: a. I *can* fix that for you right away.
　　　　　　I will be able to fix that for you right away.
　　　　　b. You *should* have taken care of that matter a long time ago.
　　　　　　You ought to have taken care of that matter a long time ago.
　　　　　c. I *must* pay this bill before the end of the month.
　　　　　　I have to pay (informal I've got to pay) this bill before the end of the month.
　　　　　d. *Must* you leave so soon?
　　　　　　Do you have to leave so soon? or Have you got to leave so soon?
　　　　　e. Even as a child, he *would* sit and write poetry for hours.
　　　　　　Even as a child, he used to sit and write poetry for hours.
　　　　　f. All the salesgirls *are required to* dress neatly.
　　　　　　All the salesgirls are to dress neatly.

1. I *must* see him now.

_____

2. When he was young, he *would* go for a long walk every morning.

_____

3. You *are supposed to* hand in your assignments every day.

_____

---

[12]**Used to** for past custom should not be confused with the phrase **be used to**, in which **used** is a synonym for **accustomed.**

4. His doctor told him he *should* see a heart specialist at once.

---

5. *Must* these forms be filled out right away?

---

6. Students *are required to* type their research papers.

---

7. The doctor *can* see you in a few minutes.

---

8. He *should* have worked for a living, instead of accepting his wife's money.

---

9. The usher is telling him that he *must* be quiet in the movies.

---

10. You *should* get more rest.

---

11. When he went to high school, he *wouldn't* pay any attention to his teachers.

---

12. She *couldn't* come to work because she was sick.

---

13. Everyone in the office *is required to* work overtime tonight.

---

14. He *shouldn't* have spoken to her so rudely.

---

15. Everyone *must* have food and shelter.

---

16. She *should* be doing her housework instead of gossiping with her neighbor.

---

17. He *should* be here any minute.

---

18. When he lived at the beach, *would* he go swimming often?

---

19. The announcement *was supposed to* have been made today, but so far we've heard nothing.

---

20. She *shouldn't* have put the bananas in the refrigerator.

_____

21. When he was very busy, the President *wouldn't* always write his own speeches.

_____

22. The plane *is scheduled to* arrive at Kennedy Airport.

_____

23. In your country, *would* everyone celebrate this holiday in the same way?

_____

4-14
PAST AUXILIARIES
IN SEQUENCE OF TENSES

A past main verb often requires the past tense of the verb in a dependent clause.

Present	He *is giving* a check to the boy who *delivers* the newspapers.
Past	He *gave* a check to the boy who *delivered* the newspapers.

An auxiliary used with the verb in the dependent clause is in past form.

Present	I'*m* sure that he *will regret* his rude remarks.
Past	I *was* sure that he *would regret* his rude remarks.

Change each sentence to the past tense. Be sure to use the past form of the auxiliary in the dependent clause. (Some dependent clauses have more than one verb that need to be changed.)

EXAMPLE: a. She is planting the seeds which have been given to her by a friend.
        She *planted* the seeds which *had been given* to her by a friend.
        (Note that for a single action, the simple past tense may correspond to the present progressive tense.)
     b. He tells us that he cannot come because he is ill.
        He *told* us he *could not come* because he *was* ill. (two verbs in the dependent clause)
     c. Even though he can't afford it, he is buying a new home.
        Even though he *couldn't afford* it, he *bought* a new house.

1. I don't know who will do the job.

_____

_____

2. The police believe that the child may have been kidnaped.

_____

_____

3. The company wants to hire someone who can type well.

_____

_____

4. The child's mother says that he may go back to school soon.

_____

_____

5. His teacher feels that the boy ought to be reprimanded.

_____

_____

6. They agree that no more can be done than has been done already.

_____

_____

7. We wonder why they must always come late.

_____

_____

8. They are taking the train early so that they may avoid the rush hour crowd.

_____

_____

9. He is paying the boy who has been delivering the newspapers.

_____

_____

10. The students are asking whether they may leave early the day before the holiday.

_____

_____

11. It is evident that he has been doing his best.

_____

_____

12. Because the job can't be finished on schedule, they are asking for an extension of time.

_____

_____

13. He says he must leave immediately.

_____

_____

14. Although he should be writing some letters, he is watching television instead.

_____

_____

15. We believe they must be out of town. (**Must** is used here for inference.)

_____

_____

16. We are positive that he will come to the conference.

_____

_____

17. He is working hard so that he can take a vacation soon.

_____

_____

18. There is enough room on the ship only for those who must leave the country.

_____

_____

4-15

CONTRACTIONS WITH AUXILIARIES

An auxiliary may contract not only with the negative **not** that follows it, but with the subject that precedes it. Contractions with **not** have already been taken up in the preceding chapter under negatives and questions. Contractions with the subject take the following form:

be		have		shall-will	
am —	**'m**	has —	**'s**	shall—will —	**'ll**
is —	**'s**	have —	**'ve**	should—would —	**'d**
are —	**'re**	had —	**'d**		

Contractions with subjects do not occur with the auxiliary **do** or with modal auxiliaries.

Contractions with Subjects

Wherever possible, use a contraction between the subject and the auxiliary.

1. She is leaving on Saturday.

_____

2. I shall miss you.

_____

3. What have you got there?

_____

4. They were stopped at the border.

_____

5. Please see who is at the door.[13]

_____

6. Who has the starring role in that movie?[13]

_____

7. I had hoped to get here earlier, but my train was delayed.

_____

8. She was late to work this morning.

_____

9. Whom did they choose?

_____

10. What will your friends think about your rash behavior?

_____

11. I am not eager to finish school quickly.

_____

12. How will you pay for that car?

_____

13. The paper has finally arrived.

_____

14. I should like to hear from you.

_____

[13]The independent verb **be** may contract with the subject, but not the independent verb **have.**

15. You should be hearing from him soon.[14]

_____

16. He would appreciate any help you can give him.

_____

Contractions with Subjects or with NOT

Generally, except for the auxiliaries **am**, **is**, **are**, contractions with subjects are less likely than contractions with **not**.

Wherever possible, contract the auxiliary with both the subject and with **not**.

EXAMPLE: a. He is not planning to go to the party.
   He's not planning to go to the party. _____
   He isn't planning to go to the party. _____
b. I am not going to see him.
   I'm not going to see him.[15] _____

1. They are not impressed by his record.

_____

_____

2. We were not allowed to enter the hospital room.

_____

_____

3. The girl was not in a hurry to leave.

_____

_____

4. The train has not arrived yet.[16]

_____

_____

5. The children have not eaten dinner yet.[16]

_____

_____

[14]No contraction occurs when **should** is the equivalent of the modal auxiliary **ought to**.
[15]**Ain't** is an illiterate contraction for **am not**.
[16]Contractions between noun subjects and auxiliaries represent very informal usage.

6. She had not seen the car coming.

_____

_____

7. I shall not see him today.

_____

_____

8. He will not permit this to happen again.

_____

_____

9. I should not like to be poor.

_____

_____

10. They would not enjoy that movie.

_____

_____

11. We cannot deny that he is charming.

_____

_____

12. He said he could not enter the contest.

_____

_____

13. He might not find the street without a map.

_____

_____

14. You must not say such things.

_____

_____

15. She had not been warned about his bad temper.

_____

_____

16. I do not think he will come.

_____

_____

4-16
DO AS AUXILIARY

The **do** auxiliary is accompanied by the simple form of the verb. It is used only in the *simple present* tense (**do** or **does offer**) and in the *simple past* tense (**did offer**).

Questions	***Do*** you like my new hat?
Negative statements	I ***don't*** like your new hat.
Abridgment—omission or substitution	I don't like coffee and neither **does** my wife. Mary works harder than her sister **does**.
Emphasis	My teacher thinks I didn't study for my test, but I **did** study. The letter we were expecting never **did** arrive.

Supply **do**, **does**, or **did**.

1. How much _____ these shoes cost?

2. What _____ you buy yesterday?

3. Where _____ he go last night?

4. Why _____ you think he won't come tonight?

5. What _____ this word mean?

6. I _____ n't get any sleep at all last night.

7. He never _____ get to the station last night.

8. I _____ n't remember what his name is.

9. She _____ n't want his help now.

10. We _____ n't get your letter in time to meet you at the airport.

11. We often serve dinner outdoors, and so _____ our neighbors.

12. He likes to watch football on television, but his wife _____ n't.

13. The owner of the factory worked just as hard as his employees _____ in order to get the order out on time.

14. Although I have little time for entertainment, I _____ go to the theater once in a while.

15. He _____ have money, but it's all tied up in property.

16. How long _____ it generally take to fly from the East Coast to the West Coast?

17. They never go to bed before midnight and neither _____ their children.

18. She claims she can't cook, but she really _____ know how.

19. Everyone in the office worked late, and I _____ too.

4-17

REVIEW OF AUXILIARIES

Use the required auxiliary with each verb. In some sentences there are two possibilities.

EXAMPLE: a. My friend always wears very expensive dresses to school. Her parents (have) _____must have_____ a lot of money.

b. I (take) _____should take_____ better care of my garden, but I don't have enough time.

c. He said there was a possibility that the concert (call off) _____might (*or* would) be called off_____ .

d. My cold is getting worse. I (stay) _____had better (*or* should) stay_____ home today.

1. We (get) _____ to the airport by nine o'clock; otherwise we'll miss our plane.

2. When I was a youngster, I (not worry) _____ about anything at all.

3. No one (live) _____ without food.

4. I (prepare) _____ my income tax return last month, but I kept putting it off. Now I (do) _____ it if I don't want to pay a penalty for filing late.

5. (I help) _____ you clear the table?

6. His secretary asked whether she (have) _____ the afternoon off to do some shopping.

7. There is no more paper left, so I (not continue) _____ typing.

8. Any one of the three suspects (commit) _____ the murder yesterday.

9. He (be) _____ thankful that he wasn't hurt in that accident instead of complaining about the damage to his car.

10. He was warned that he (pay) _____ the fine or that he (put) _____ in prison.

11. This wine is excellent. You (try) _____ it.

12. He (eat) _____ less if he wants to lose weight.

13. I (see) _____ you at once. I have important news for you.

14. You (not listen) _____ to him. He will only cause you trouble.

15. I (pay) _____ this bill immediately or I will be charged additional interest.

16. All the necessary documents (file) _____ within the next week.

17. The authorities are trying to determine what (cause) _____ the plane crash.

18. We're almost out of bread. We (buy) _____ some more right away.

19. The doctor said that the patient (need) _____ an operation if his condition got any worse.

20. I don't know what the trouble is. They (be) _____ here long before now.

21. You (not make) _____ such sarcastic remarks to him when you saw him yesterday.

22. He (be) _____ very hungry now because he has had nothing to eat all day.

23. He asked his broker whether he (buy) _____ those stocks.

24. He (recover) _____ from his illness if he had really wanted to live.

25. They (decide) _____ not to come to the party; otherwise they (already be) _____ here.

26. (You always talk) _____ about the same subject? I find it very boring.

27. (I make) _____ the beds first or (I wash) _____ _____ the dishes first?

28. It's not raining so hard now. It (clear up) _____ in a little while.

5

Adjectives

STRUCTURAL DESCRIPTION OF ADJECTIVES

Function	Form	Markers
Modifies a noun ***beautiful*** *girls*	Grammatical endings for comparison *-er, -est*	For comparison *more, most*
Modifies a pronoun *They are* ***beautiful****;* *something* ***new***	Derivational endings *-ous, -ic(al), -al,* *-ant* or *-ent, -ible* or *-able,-ful, -less,* *-y, -ish, -some,* etc.	intensifiers of degree *very, so, quite,* *too,* etc.

Position

1. *Before a noun*

Determiners		Descriptive adjectives			Noun adjuncts
articles *a, the*	numerals *first three,* *last ten,* etc.	general description *beautiful,* *intelligent,* *clear,* etc.	physical state size—*large* shape—*oval* age—*old* temperature— *cold* color—*red*	proper adjective nationality— *Irish* religion— *Catholic*	*college* (student) *gasoline* (station)
demonstratives *this, that*					
possessives *my, your*					
adjectives of indefinite quantity *some, much,* etc.					

2. *After a verb*
   a. after linking verbs (*be, seem, appear, look, become*)
      She is ***beautiful****.*
   b. in objective complement position (*make, consider, keep*)
      His behavior made me ***uneasy****.*

5-1
SEQUENCE OF DETERMINERS

Determiners may be broken up into three groups—pre-determiners, the determiners themselves, and post-determiners. All of these may be preceded by intensifiers of the entire noun phrase.[1]

Intensifiers (adverbs) 1	Pre-determiners 2	Determiners 3	Post-determiners (numbers) 4		
even	both[2]	the, a	*Ordinal*	*Cardinal*	
only	all[2]	this, that	*4a*	*4b*	*4bb*
just	half[2]	my, John's	first	one	other
		etc.	second	two	more
			third	three	
			etc.	etc.	
		indefinite adjectives			
	multipliers	*3a* *3b*	*sequence adjectives*		
	twice	several other	last		
	double	some more	next		
	triple	any	following		
	many times	either			
	ten times	every			
	etc.	each			
		much			
		many			
		(a) few			
		(a) little			
		(the) less			
		(the) least			
		(the) most			

Note that **other** and **more** may be used not only after other indefinite adjectives (**several other people, many more books**), but after cardinal numbers (**three other people, two more books**).

Few follows **the first, the last, the next** (**the first few years, the next few days**).

Arrange the determiners in the proper order.

1. (the, both) girls were sent to camp.

_____

2. (two, only, more) napkins are needed.

_____

[1]A noun phrase is the noun head with its preceding and following modification.
[2]**Both, all, half** may also be followed by **of**—**both (of) his children.**

3. (first, Mary's, two) English teachers were very good.

_____

4. He ordered (more, dozen, a) roses than he did last time.

_____

5. (most, other) men would have done it differently.

_____

6. The children were placed in (other, every) seat for the examination.

_____

7. (two, first, the) men refused; (the, other, two)[3] men said they would consider the offer.

_____

8. (next, the, few) years will see many changes.

_____

9. In (few, a, more) days we will be leaving for California.

_____

10. He had (many, too, other) places to visit to stay there long.

_____

11. (few, the, first) pages were spoiled.

_____

12. He claims he needs (more, some) money; however, he has (much, more) money than he will admit.

_____

13. (triple, the, even) appropriations granted last year will not be sufficient now.

_____

14. (last, these, few) days have been very busy ones.

_____

15. (the, half, only) concert hall was filled.[4]

_____

16. (more, many) people came than were expected.

_____

17. I have (half, just, a)[5] tank of gasoline left.

_____

[3]**Other** may precede or follow a cardinal numeral.

[4]**Only** is an intensifier of the entire noun phrase. In the sense of _one_, **only** may appear before **the**—the _only_ other person in the room; the _only_ way to do it.

[5]**Half a** or **a half** may be used.

5-2

SEQUENCE OF ADJECTIVES BEFORE NOUNS

Determiners 1	*Descriptive Adjectives* 2			*Noun Adjuncts* 3	*Nouns*
	general description	physical state	proper adjective		
		(size, shape, age, temperature, color)	*(nationality, religion, etc.)* *(also some adjectives ending in -ic(al), -al, etc.)*		
both the	air-conditioned	white	Lincoln Continental		cars
a	beautiful, exclusive		residential		district
those three	self-conscious	little old			ladies
Jane's	daringly-cut		Parisian	evening	gown
a		very large	Buddhist		temple
that	temperamental		Italian	opera	singer

Commas generally appear only between two or more adjectives of general description. Commas between adjectives of general description and physical state are often optional.

The position of adjectives of general description and of physical state may sometimes be reversed.

Rewrite the following, arranging the words in parentheses in the proper order. Use commas where necessary.

1. (angry, those, young, all) men

_____

2. (lively, black and white, a, little) kitten

_____

3. (muddy, steep, a, river) bank

_____

4. (self-centered, those, old) Frenchmen

_____

5. (bone, white, exquisitely designed) china

_____

6. (recent, stormy, wet, this) weather

_____

7. (Italian, a, young, light-hearted) schoolgirl

_____

8. (ivory, little, intricately carved) figurines

_____

9. (sympathetic, that, young, English) teacher

_____

10. (white, expensive, Steinway, the teacher's) piano

_____

11. (gifted, young, college, Negro) students

_____

12. (old, American, two, colonial, spacious) houses

_____

13. (commercial, the, first, jet, ten) planes

_____

14. (aluminum, multi-purpose, kitchen, four) utensils

_____

15. (well-known, Catholic, several, French) priests

_____

16. (brand-new, expensive, an, four-lane) highway

_____

17. (small, very spoiled, two, French, black) poodles

_____

5-3
PROPER ADJECTIVES
ADJECTIVES OF NATIONALITY

Proper nouns and adjectives refer to nationalities, geographical places, religions, holidays, dates, names of people or organizations, titles, etc. Such words always begin with capital letters.

Proper noun	Proper adjective
Italy	**Italian** food
Paris	**Parisian** styles
Christianity	**Christian** beliefs
Arab	**Arabian** nights

Give the adjective used for each country. Then give the noun for a person coming from that country. Be sure to begin each word of nationality with a capital letter.

Germany   a ___German___ custom   He is a ___German___ .

Japan   a ___Japanese___ custom   He is a ___Japanese___ .

Ireland   an ___Irish___ custom   He is an ___Irishman___ .

Egypt   an _____ custom   He is an _____ .

Poland   a _____ custom   He is a _____ .

India   an _____ custom   He is an _____ .

Scotland   a _____ custom   He is a _____ .

Holland   a _____ custom   He is a _____ .

Brazil   a _____ custom   He is a _____ .

Russia   a _____ custom   He is a _____ .

France   a _____ custom   He is a _____ .

Canada   a _____ custom   He is a _____ .

Israel   an _____ custom   He is an _____ .

Spain   a _____ custom   He is a _____ .

Venezuela   a _____ custom   He is a _____ .

Turkey   a _____ custom   He is a _____ .

the United States   an _____ custom   He is an _____ .

Australia   an _____ custom   He is an _____ .

Hungary   a _____ custom   He is a _____ .

Greece   a _____ custom   He is a _____ .

Cuba   a _____ custom   He is a _____ .

5-4
COMPARISON OF ADJECTIVES

| -er _____ than comparative |
| the _____ -est superlative |

| more _____ than comparative |
| the most _____ superlative |

1. *adjectives with one syllable:*
   taller than, the tallest
2. *adjectives with two syllables ending in:*
   -y   **dirtier than, the dirtiest**
   -le **nobler than, the noblest**

1. *adjectives with three or more syllables:*
   more beautiful than, the most beautiful
2. *two-syllable adjectives with derivational endings (-ful, -less, -ish, -ous, -ing, -ed, etc.):*
   more useful than, the most useful

Two-syllable adjectives with either form:
1. adjectives ending in -er—**clever, tender, bitter**
2. adjectives ending in -ow—**narrow, shallow, mellow**
3. adjectives ending in -some—**handsome, wholesome, lonesome**
4. others—**polite, profound, sincere, severe, common, pleasant, cruel, quiet, stupid**

Irregular comparison:

1. Positive	2. Comparative	3. Superlative
good	**better**	**best**
bad	**worse**	**worst**
far	**farther** (for distance—formal)	**farthest**
	further (for addition)	**furthest**
little	**less**	**least**
much **many**	**more**	**most**

In adding **-er** or **-est** for comparison, keep in mind that:

1. Final *y* preceded by a consonant is changed to *i*—**livelier, tastier, luckier.**
2. A final single consonant preceded by a single vowel is doubled—**bigger, thinner, hottest.**
3. Finel *e* is dropped—**simpler, largest, wider.**

Supply the comparative or superlative form of the adjective.

EXAMPLE: a. He is (greedy) _____ the greediest _____ man I have ever met.
b. The weather in Florida is (hot) _____ hotter than _____ the weather in my native country.

1. It is (good) _____ to give _____ to receive.

2. She is (helpless) _____ person I have ever known.

3. They are looking for a (big) _____ apartment _____ the one they now have.

4. He is by far (bad) _____ student in his class.

5. Some people arc (reliable) _____ others.

6. He is much (familiar) _____ with modern painting _____ with modern music.

7. (Difficult) _____ job of all still remains to be done.

8. His works are far (creative) _____ those of his contemporaries.

9. He is (lively) _____ of all the children in the class.

10. Although he is a world-famous scientist, he is (modest) _____ _____ most men.

11. She earns much (little) _____ money _____ her husband does.

12. If he ever gets out of his country he will try to live in (free) _____ land in the world.

13. The recipes in my cookbook are (simple) _____ the ones in your cookbook.

14. This library has far (many) _____ books _____ any library I have ever been in.

15. There is a belief that professors are absent-minded, but I have known some people who are much (absent-minded) _____ any professors.

16. This fan is (noisy) _____ the one we had before.

5-5
DERIVATION (1)
ADDING ADJECTIVE SUFFIXES TO WORDS
THAT END IN SILENT *E*

		exceptions
*Keep the **e** before a consonant*	careful hopeless lively	awful *after **u**—*duly, truly
*Drop the **e** before a vowel (including **y**)*	desirable nervous practical observant noisy	*after **c** or **g**—* noticeable, manageable (*to keep the sound "soft" before **a**, **o**, **u***)

Add the designated adjective suffixes to the words given below.

lone + ly _____   life + less _____

admire + able _____   observe + ant _____

use + less _____   shame + ful _____

excuse + able _____   imagine + ary _____

true + ly _____   outrage + ous _____

peace + ful _____   hypocrite + ical _____

value + able _____   waste + ful _____

change + able _____   awe + ful _____

juice + y _____   replace + able _____

courage + ous _____   love + able[6] _____

notice + able _____   grace + ious _____

5-6
DERIVATION (2)
CHANGING Y TO I

Final *y* becomes *i* before an added consonant or vowel.

colony + al = colonial
mercy + ful = merciful

Add the designated adjective suffixes to the words given below.

mystery + ous _____   day + ly _____

mercy + less _____   beauty + ful _____

rely + able _____   family + ar _____

envy + ous _____   pity + ful _____

colony + al _____   envy + able _____

industry + ous _____   plenty + ful _____

ceremony + al _____   victory + ous _____

[6]A few **-able** adjectives derived from one-syllable verbs may be spelled with or without the *e*—**us(e)able, lik(e)able, lov(e)able, sal(e)able.** The spelling with *e* is less common.

DERIVATION (3)
DOUBLING FINAL CONSONANTS
BEFORE ADJECTIVE SUFFIXES

one-syllable word			rót	t	en
two-three syllable word		re	grét	t	able
	un	con	tról	l	able

Exceptions: éxcellent, transférable

Note that: 1) the added adjective suffix *begins with a vowel*; 2) the syllable before the adjective suffix ends in a *single consonant preceded by a single vowel*; and 3) the syllable before the added adjective suffix is *stressed*.

The same rule applies if the adjective suffix -*y* is added.

Use the appropriate adjective. Be careful of the spelling.

1. The pavement is very (slip) _____ because of last night's heavy rain.

2. Some of the newly rich are more (snob) _____ than those whose families have been wealthy for a long time.

3. His piano recital was truly an (unforget) _____ experience.

4. The day was so (fog) _____ that you couldn't see a thing in front of you.

5. That was a (regret) _____ incident. Please accept our apologies.

6. Student groups all over the world are becoming more (rebel) _____ against authority.

7. He wears clothes that are casual, almost slovenly; his trousers are always (bag) _____ .

8. This wine is (excel) _____ .

9. These passes are not (transfer) _____ ; they may be used only by the persons to whom they were issued.

10. All the strawberries in this box are (rot) _____ .

11. I don't think that comedian was very (fun). _____ .

12. She seems to prefer (man) _____ clothes to feminine ones.

13. After the heavy rains the roads became so (mud) _____ that they couldn't be used.

Adjectives from Nouns
(-y, -ly, (i)al, -ous, -ic(al),
-ish, -like, -ary or -ery, -ful, -less, -wide)

Give the adjective forms of the nouns in parentheses. Make whatever spelling changes are necessary.

1. The name Philadelphia stands for the "City of (Brother) _____ Love."

2. She has always behaved in a (duty) _____ way toward her parents.

3. There's a cold wind blowing; I feel very (chill) _____.

4. A Cadillac car is so (cost) _____ that most people cannot afford one.

5. Some neurotic people become (hysteria) _____ over any little emotional disturbance.

6. His recent religious conversion has made him so (piety) _____ that he is forever praying and fasting.

7. Remarks that sound as though they come out of a book are (book) _____.

8. It was very (courage) _____ of him to risk his life trying to save a drowning child.

9. The damage to this painting is so extensive that the painting is almost (value) _____.

10. A portrait that looks almost like the original is very (life) _____.

Adjectives from Verbs
(-ent or -ant, -able or -ible, -ive, -ed, -ing,
-some, -ile, -(at)ory, -worthy)

Supply the correct adjective endings to the underlined verb forms. Make whatever spelling changes are necessary.

1. He won't go away. He's very (persist) _____ about seeing you.

2. Excessive smoking and drinking are (destroy) _____ of one's health.

3. He was so (persuade) _____ that the committee all agreed to accept his proposal.

4. In a few states, first degree murder is (punish) _____ by death in the electric chair.

5. He is very (hesitate) _____ about taking such a long trip.

6. It soon became (appear) _____ that he was lying.

7. Don't throw that tire away. It's still (service) _____.

8. What is so (amaze) _____ is that no one was seriously hurt in that car accident.

9. Parents like their children to be (obey) _____.

10. I have walked too much; my ankles have become (swell) _____.

5-9
DERIVATION (5)

Supply the adjective forms that are required because of the preceding italicized words.

EXAMPLE: a. The dancer's *flexibility* of movement is remarkable. I never thought that a person could be so _____flexible_____.

b. He has great *sympathy* for his fellowmen. Such a _____sympathetic_____ man is hard to find.

1. His parents *permit* him to do whatever he pleases. This _____ attitude is certainly going to spoil the child.

2. This registration form doesn't require an *explanation*. It is self-_____.

3. This house has a great deal of *space* to put things. We were lucky to find such a _____ house.

4. Those two men have been *quarreling* for some time. They are both very _____.

5. I hope I did not *offend* you. I would not like to be _____ to you in any way.

6. There is sometimes a great difference between *theory* (1) and *practice* (2). _____ (1) knowledge is often useless unless it can be applied in a _____ (2) way.

7. He does everything with great *enthusiasm* (1). No one can accuse him of *apathy* (2). A person who is _____ (1) gets much more work done than one who is _____ (2).

8. He spoke with great *force* (1) and *vigor* (2). But he could not *persuade* (3) the committee, because an argument, besides being _____ (1) and _____ (2), can be _____ (3) only if it is backed by facts.

9. She always has a guilty *conscience* if she doesn't do things in a _____ way.

10. People who do things according to an orderly *system* are _____.

11. You've made a great *number* of mistakes on this report; they're too _____ to be overlooked.

5-10
-ING, -ED, ADJECTIVES (1)

Use the **-ing**, **-ed** adjectives as in the example.

EXAMPLE: *The game excited the audience.*

The game was _____exciting_____   The audience was _____excited_____

The _____exciting_____ game   The _____excited_____ audience

(*active* force —the **-ing** adjective goes with the   (*passive* force —the **-ed** adjective goes with the
original *subject* of a sentence)   original *object* of a sentence)

1. *The work tired the boy.*

The work was _____   The boy was _____

The _____ work   The _____ boy

2. *The lecture bored the students.*

The lecture was _____   The students were _____

The _____ lecture   The _____ students

3. *The experience disappointed the men.*

The experience was _____   The men were _____

The _____ experience   The _____ men

4. *The teacher's display of anger astonished the children.*

The teacher's display of anger was _____   The children were _____

The teacher's _____ display of anger   The _____ children

5. *The sight of a bear nearby terrified the campers.*

The sight of a bear nearby was _____   The campers were _____

The _____ sight of a bear nearby   The _____ campers

6. *The chemical substance purified the water.*

The chemical substance was _____   The water was _____.

The _____ chemical substance   The _____ water.

-ING, -ED, ADJECTIVES (2)

Supply the correct participial adjective. Use the test **The** _____ **is** *or* **was** _____. (Some of the past participial adjectives may be irregular.)

EXAMPLE: a. That was the most (thrill) _____thrilling_____ experience I have ever had.
(The experience was thrilling.)

b. The (defeat) _____defeated_____ army laid down their arms.
(The army was defeated.)

1. The young writer was pleased with the editor's (encourage) _____ remarks.

2. Such an experiment is valid only under rigidly (control) _____ conditions.

3. The (attack) _____ forces laid siege to the city for a long time.

4. The (shock) _____ news of her son's death caused her to sob uncontrollably.

5. She is a very (fascinate) _____ woman.

6. The (disgust) _____ critic left the theater long before the end of the wretched play.

7. He made a (surprise) _____ financial recovery after his bankruptcy.

8. His disease is already in a very (advance) _____ state.

9. The Salvation Army collects (discard) _____ clothes and household goods.

10. Spices and herbs act as (flavor) _____ agents.

11. The (wash) _____ and (iron) _____ clothes should be put in this drawer.

12. She is throwing out all her (tear) _____ or (stain) _____ linen.

13. The pictures will be taken by a (hide) _____ camera.

14. The (speed) _____ car ran recklessly along the (twist) _____ mountain road.

15. A (break) _____ spring caused all the trouble.

16. To see a (love) _____ mother and a (smile) _____ baby is a (reward) _____ experience.

17. He drove a (rent) _____ car to the (desert) _____ house, but the (lock) _____ door prevented him from getting in.

18. Ice cream and sherbet are (freeze) _____ desserts.

5-12
MUCH-MANY, (A) LITTLE—(A) FEW, LESS—FEWER

Noncountable Noun	Plural Countable Noun
Much furniture **is** needed. (A) **Little** furniture **is** needed. **Less** furniture **is** needed.	**Many** chairs **are** needed. (A) **Few** chairs **are** needed. **Fewer**[7] chairs **are** needed.

A little, a few stress the *presence* of something in a small quantity (**I have a little money; I have a few friends**); **little, few** stress the *absence* of almost all quantity (**I have little money; I have few friends**).

Underline the correct forms.

EXAMPLE: a. There (was, <u>were</u>) (much, <u>many</u>) accidents on the wet road.

  b. (<u>Much</u>, many) more information (<u>is</u>, are) necessary before we can write up the report. (**Much** or **many** may function as an intensifier of **more**.)

1. There is (much, many) more beautiful scenery in the mountains than in the plains.
2. (Little, a little) soap (is, are) all we will need.
3. (Much, many) students (was, were) hurt in the riot.
4. I still have (little, a little) money left, enough to go to the movies.
5. (Much, many) more electrical appliances (is, are) being used in the home now than (was, were) used only a decade ago.
6. Only (a few, few) trees (was, were) damaged in the storm.
7. There (is, are) (much, many) baggage in the luggage compartment of the train.
8. (Fewer, less) children get polio today than in the past.
9. (Much, many) news (is, are) being broadcast over the radio and on television.
10. How (much, many) clothing are you taking for your trip?
11. There (is, are) (much, many) advertising in American newspapers.
12. Educated people use (little, few) slang.
13. How (much, many) machines (is, are) in operation now?
14. (Much, many) expensive machinery (is, are) required to do the job.
15. You have made too (much, many) mistakes on this paper.
16. There (was, were) very (much, many) people on the excursion boat.
17. Only (few, a few) decades ago, most people did not have TV sets.
18. Even late at night you can find (few, a few) people still working at their desks.
19. (Few, a few) people have ever entered his home.
20. How (much, many) slices of toast would you like?

[7]In informal speech **less** is also used with plural nouns—**less chairs.**

Some, any represent an indefinite amount. **Some** is used in positive statements, **any** in negative statements.

> I have **some** money.
> I don't have **any** money.

Some or **any** may be used with questions.

> Do you have **any** money? (at all)
> Do you have **some** money? (at least a small quantity)

Any used in a positive statement means *it doesn't matter which*—**Any clerk in the store can help you.**

Supply some or any.

EXAMPLE: a. We need _____ some _____ thumbtacks to put this notice up on the bulletin
board. Do you have _____ any _____?

1. There were _____ oranges here a few minutes ago.

2. There aren't _____ glasses on the table.

3. Do you want _____ fruit for dessert?

4. _____ books are lying on the table.

5. Which book do you want? _____ one will do.

6. Please buy me _____ stamps at the post office.

7. The store doesn't have _____ electric fans now. They will
have _____ in a few days.

8. We don't expect to meet _____-one we know on our trip.

9. Only _____-body with experience can handle this job.

10. _____ teller in the bank can take care of you.

11. _____-one caught cheating on the examination will be
expelled from school.

12. Not _____-one can do this work; it requires intelligence
and speed.

13. Give this package to _____-one who comes to the door.

14. Everyone was asked to contribute _____-thing, but he
didn't give _____-thing.

15. He refused to take _____ compensation for the work he
had done.

5-14
ADJECTIVES USED
IN THE COMPARISON OF NOUNS

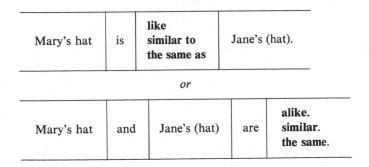

Mary's hat	is	like similar to the same as	Jane's (hat).

or

Mary's hat	and	Jane's (hat)	are	alike. similar. the same.

The same may also immediately precede the noun—**Mary is wearing the same hat as Jane.**

Supply the proper adjectives for the comparisons of nouns made in the following sentences. Use the same number of words as there are blanks.

EXAMPLE: a. Your car is _____the_____ _____same_____ _____as_____ mine. The two cars are _____the_____ _____same_____ .

b. The coat you just bought is _____like_____ the one I bought last year. The two coats are _____alike_____ .

1. His income and that of his wife are _____ _____ . His income is _____ _____ _____ that of his wife.

2. He told a story _____ the one his father did. The two stories were very much _____ .

3. Our house is just _____ our neighbor's. The two houses are _____ .

4. The styles today are _____ _____ the styles worn some time ago.

5. It doesn't matter which typewriter you use. They're both _____ .

6. The suit he's wearing now is _____ _____ the one I'm wearing. The two suits are _____ .

7. They both do _____ _____ kind of work.

8. This lake is _____ _____ the lake I used to swim in when I was a child. The two lakes are _____ .

9. Vegetables from the store are not _____ _____ _____ vegetables from the garden.

6

Articles

The (definite article)	*A* (indefinite article)
Developed from a word meaning **this**. Signals a *particular* person or thing—*the student sitting next to you*. Used with singular or plural nouns.	Developed from a word meaning **one**. **An** used before vowel sounds. Signals an *unspecified* one of others—*a student sitting in the front row*. Used chiefly with singular countable nouns.

Uses of the Articles

1. For known persons or objects in the environment
   *He walked into **the** house and hung his coat in **the** closet.*
2. For persons, things or ideas particularized by the verbal context
   a. preceding context—***A** strange dog came onto the porch. **The** dog seemed very friendly.*
   b. following context—***The** man **standing near the window** will be our guest speaker tonight.*
3. For a class as a whole
   ***The** lion is an animal.*
4. With a "ranking" adjective
   ***the** best way*; ***the** fifth lesson*
5. With nouns or gerunds + **of** phrases
   ***the** election of officers*
   ***the** changing of the guards*
6. In **of** phrases after words of quantity
   *most of **the** men in the factory*
   *four of **the** children from that school*
7. For place names
   ***the** Mississippi River*
   ***the** Alps*

1. In the sense of *one*, or *each*
   *I waited **an** hour.*
   *His rent is $200 **a** month.*
2. For an unidentified member of a class
   *We saw **a** lion at the zoo.*
3. For a representative member of a class
   a. identifying an individual member
      *That animal is **a** lion.*
   b. defining a smaller class
      *The lion is **an** animal.*

An is used before a word beginning with a vowel *sound*.

> an apple, an accident
> an hour, but a horrible event
> a university, but an unusual event

Use **a** or **an** before the following words.

_____ argument

_____ unavoidable delay

_____ half hour

_____ union

_____ heiress

_____ humiliating experience

_____ herb

_____ ugly child

_____ happily married woman

_____ unique opportunity

_____ accident

_____ helicopter

_____ uninvited guest

_____ universal feeling

_____ historical occasion

_____ underdeveloped country

_____ human being

_____ unit

_____ garage

_____ holiday

_____ umbrella

_____ hourly application

_____ useful gadget

_____ honest man

_____ unlooked-for blessing

_____ yellow dress

_____ humid day

_____ unanimous decision

_____ huge tree

_____ unfamiliar situation

_____ humorous story

_____ hospital

_____ humble man

_____ honorable person

6-2
ARTICLE vs. NO ARTICLE (1)

An article is required with a singular countable noun.

I need _____ furniture
I need _____ chairs
I need _____ the *or* a _____ chair

The article is required even if a descriptive adjective accompanies the singular countable noun.

I need a comfortable chair.

However, if a determiner other than the article accompanies the noun, the article is not used.

I need this (or my, another, one) chair.

Supply the article **a** if it is required.

EXAMPLE: a. He requested _____ a _____ prompt reply to his letter.

  b. He deserves _____ — _____ admiration for his work.

  c. There will be _____ a _____ brief pause for intermission.

1. He does not have _____ single regret about what he did.

2. She likes to eat _____ good food.

3. He made _____ bad mistake in his report.

4. He has accumulated _____ great wealth from his investments.

5. He speaks with _____ great authority on the subject.

6. He is consulting with _____ authority on urban development.

7. She wants to become _____ nurse.

8. They asked him _____ difficult question.

9. _____ honesty and _____ loyalty are rare virtues.

10. After the sun set, _____ darkness closed in very fast.

11. _____ youngster was hit by _____ car while he was crossing the street.

12. What _____ bad weather we are having today.

13. He wants to hire _____ good housekeeper.

14. The lawyer gave his client _____ very good advice.

6-3
ARTICLE vs. NO ARTICLE (2)

The is often used with a noncountable noun *when the noun is followed by a modifier.*

The milk ⎰ which I bought a few days ago ⎱ should still be good.
       ⎨ left over from yesterday ⎬
       ⎰ in the refrigerator ⎱

but   Milk is good for children.
       Fresh milk tastes good.

Supply the article **the** if it is required.

1. _____ genius of Edison is universally recognized.

2. _____ genius is 10% inspiration and 90% perspiration.

3. _____ bread has been called the staff of life.

4. _____ bread you baked is delicious.

5. _____ silver is used for money and jewelry.

6. _____ silver in this ring is of inferior quality.

7. He is studying _____ religion.

8. I would like to know more about _____ strange religion of these primitive people.

9. In order to survive, we must all have _____ food and _____ water.

10. _____ food in the restaurant near me is fairly good.

11. _____ water used in this beer comes from a special spring.

12. _____ psychology of birds and animals would be an interesting subject to study.

13. _____ psychology tells us a great deal about _____ human nature.

14. _____ smoke coming from the forest fire can be seen for miles around.

15. Where there's _____ smoke, there's _____ fire.

16. _____ baseball is the favorite sport of most Americans.

17. The American Constitution guarantees _____ life, _____ liberty, and _____ pursuit of happiness.

18. _____ transportation of troops to the troubled area took a long time.

19. _____ transportation has always been a problem in that area because of the bad roads.

6-4
GENERIC USE OF ARTICLES

In a general statement, it is possible to use **the**, **a**, or no article with a concrete countable noun that represents a class.

The	*The* lion is a wild animal.	**The** emphasizes the *class itself*, without regard for concrete representatives of the class.
A	*A* lion is a wild animal.	**A** emphasizes an individual representative of a class. It has the sense of *any*.
No article	*Lions* are wild animals.	The plural form without an article emphasizes *all* the representatives of this class.

Use **the**, **a**, or no article before the underlined nouns in the following general statements. (In some sentences, two choices are possible.)

EXAMPLE: a. Because of _____the_____ automobile, man has extended his horizons, but he has poisoned the atmosphere.

b. _____An_____ automobile is a necessity today.

c. _____The_____ refrigerator has enabled people to keep food fresh for a much longer time.

1. _____ vegetables are good for the health.

2. The world is getting smaller because of _____ airplane.

3. _____ wheel and _____ plow were very important inventions.

4. _____ giraffe has a long neck.

5. _____ supermarket sells not only _____ groceries, but also _____ household items, _____ liquor, _____ plants, _____ magazines, and _____ candy.

6. _____ newspaper is one of the most widespread media of communication.

7. _____ tranquilizers, _____ sleeping pills, and _____ headache remedies are becoming part of our daily lives.

8. _____ computer is doing much of the work that used to be done by _____ human beings.

9. _____ engineer must have a good knowledge of mathematics and physics.

10. _____ university is a place where both _____ student and _____ teacher learn.

11. It has been proven that _____ cigarettes are bad for the health.

12. _____ eagle is a bird of prey.

The occurs with names for familiar persons or objects in the home and the community. It is also used with names for natural objects in the world and in the universe. In these uses, **the** limits a noun to the one specimen *we are familiar with or that we have in mind*, although other specimens in the class may exist.

He walked into **the** house and hung his coat in **the** closet.
As she was strolling along **the** street she looked at **the** clothes in **the** store windows.
They were sailing along **the** river watching **the** clouds in **the** sky.

In the following sentences, use **the** or **a**. Keep in mind that **a** refers to an unknown or unspecified person or thing, and that it is generally not used with a noncountable noun.

EXAMPLE: a. She ran into _____the_____ house and shut _____the_____ door.

　　　　　　b. They are planning to buy _____a_____ house some day.

1. We have to feed _____ dog and _____ cat before we leave.

2. The boy has always wanted to have _____ dog and _____ cat.

3. This apartment has _____ bedroom, _____ living room, and _____ kitchen.

4. While he was in _____ park, he saw _____ man walking with _____ dog.

5. Everyone in _____ neighborhood was sorry to see them move.

6. They moved to _____ very quiet neighborhood.

7. _____ moon waxes and wanes during the period of a month.

8. _____ heavy rain caused a great deal of damage to _____ crops.

9. Please put _____ butter, _____ bread, and _____ eggs in _____ refrigerator.

10. _____ refrigerator like theirs is very expensive.

11. He's going to _____ grocery store to buy _____ loaf of _____ bread.

12. They live in _____ very expensive home.

13. _____ moon is _____ satellite of _____ earth.

14. He would rather swim in _____ ocean than in
_____ sea.

15. She has an appointment this week with _____ doctor and
_____ dentist.

16. _____ leaves are already falling off _____
trees and covering _____ ground.

17. The drugstore hired _____ new pharmacist.

6-6
THE WITH ''RANKING'' ADJECTIVES

1. **The** plus the superlatives of adjectives

> She is *the best* cook I know.
> They bought *the most expensive* furniture in the store.
> *The richest* are not always *the happiest*.
> (Superlatives of adjectives used as nouns)

2. **The** plus ordinals

> *the fifth* row; *the ninth* day; **the third** chapter (but **chapter three**)

3. **The** plus adjectives in a time or space sequence—**the next, the following, the last**

> A student in *the last* row was asleep.

He arrived in town on Wednesday. On *the next* (or *the following*) day he gave his lecture.

> Compare with: He will give his lecture *next* week.
> He gave his lecture *last* week.

4. **The** plus other adjectives that rank nouns—**chief, principal, main, only**

> *The chief* reason for his resignation was his bad health.
> He is *the only* person who can do this job.

Give the superlative of the word in parentheses.

EXAMPLE: a. She is (lazy) student in the class.
   She is the laziest student in the class.

   b. This is (delicious) cake I have ever tasted.
   This is the most delicious cake I have ever tasted.

1. He sometimes does (childish) things I have ever seen.

_____

2. Go to see the Universal Printers; they will do (efficient) and (quick) job for you.

_____

3. (successful) people are often those who try (hard).

_____

4. (wealthy) people in the community contributed (much) money for the new wing of the hospital.

_____

Give the ordinal of the figure in parentheses.

EXAMPLE: This is (5) year we have spent our vacation here.
This is the fifth year we have spent our vacation here.

_____

1. He has almost finished writing (9) chapter.

_____

2. The meeting is scheduled for May (2). (*two possibilities*)

_____

3. She bought (2) dress she tried on.

_____

4. The office you're looking for is (3) door to the right.

_____

5. She can never do anything right (1) time.

_____

Use the, a, or no article with the word in parentheses.

EXAMPLE: This is (last) time I will ever shop in that store.
This is the last time I will ever shop in that store.

_____

1. (last) week marked the beginning of the rainy season.

_____

2. On (last) week of the sale, prices were reduced still further.

_____

3. (next) time you water the plants, give them less water.

_____

4. We are moving (next) month.

_____

5. The party lasted a long time. On (next) day everyone was tired.

_____

6. (only) excuse I can give for my rude behavior is that I was not feeling well.

_____

7. He made (only) one mistake.

_____

8. (only) restaurant that is open now is five miles from here.

_____

9. John is (only) student who didn't pass the test.

_____

10. (chief) concern of this office is with legal matters.

_____

11. (principal) exports of that country are coffee and rubber.

_____

6-7
THE WITH GERUNDS OR ABSTRACT NOUNS

The is required before gerunds or abstract nouns that are followed by **of** phrases.

gerund	**_The_** instructing **_of young children_** is difficult.
	but Instructing young children is difficult.
abstract noun	**_The_** instruction **_of young children_** is difficult.

Use **the** wherever it is required with a gerund or abstract noun that is followed by an **of** phrase.

EXAMPLE: a. _____The_____ imprisonment of people without a trial is not part of the democratic process.

b. _____—_____ imprisoning people without a trial is not part of the democratic process.

c. _____—_____ imprisonment without a trial is not part of the democratic process.

1. _____ corruption among officials was expected, but _____ corruption among so many was a shocking discovery.

2. _____ collection of garbage is done by the Sanitation Department.

3. His work as a sanitation employee is _____ collecting garbage.

4. _____ doing the job myself is easier than _____ explaining it.

5. He was arrested for _____ resisting a police officer in the course of his duty.

6. There was something about _____ description of the robbery by the victim that didn't seem quite right.

7. _____ active resistance of these young people to the law may result in prison terms for them.

8. _____ shutting down of the coal mines caused great hardship in the town.

9. _____ invention of the cotton gin changed the economy of the South.

10. _____ standardizing the divorce laws for all the states would be favored by many people.

11. _____ unearthing of new evidence has brought about a postponement of his trial.

6-8
THE WITH PLACE NAMES (1)
GENERAL RULES

1. **The** is used with names composed entirely or partially of common nouns. The last noun usually refers to a political union or association.

> the Soviet Union, the United Kingdom,
> the United Arab Republic, the British Commonwealth

2. **The** is used with names composed of common nouns plus proper nouns contained within **of** phrases.

> the Republic of China, the Union of South Africa, the Gulf of Mexico,
> the State of New York, the Lake of Geneva, the University of Pennsylvania

3. **The** is used with all plural names.

> the United States, the Philippine Islands,
> the Rocky Mountains, the Great Lakes, the Balkans

Supply **the** with place names wherever necessary. Be careful not to capitalize **the,** but note that words like **Republic, Gulf, Mountains** are capitalized.

1. _____ USSR stands for _____ Union of _____ Soviet Socialist Republics.

2. _____ Russia is the largest republic in _____ Soviet Union.

3. _____ United States is bordered on the east by _____ Canada and on the south by _____ Mexico and _____ Gulf of Mexico.

4. On a plateau bordering _____ Peru and _____ Bolivia is _____ Lake Titicaca, the highest navigable lake in the world.

5. _____ Netherlands is another name for _____ Holland.

6. _____ Mount Vesuvius is still an active volcano.

7. _____ United Arab Republic is the official name for _____ Egypt.

8. _____ North Pole and _____ South Pole are on either extremity of the earth's axis.

9. _____ Pyrenees are situated between _____ France and _____ Spain.

10. _____ Great Salt Lake in _____ state of Colorado is a remnant of an inland sea.

11. _____ Ivory Coast, now an independent country, was once part of _____ French West Africa.

12. _____ Mount Everest has the highest elevation in the world.

13. _____ Himalayas have been referred to as "the roof of the world."

14. _____ Philippines, like other islands in _____ Malay Archipelego, are the tops of drowned mountains protruding from the sea.

15. _____ Vatican is an independent papal state within the commune of _____ Rome.

16. The earth is divided by _____ equator into _____ Northern Hemisphere and _____ Southern Hemisphere.

17. _____ Persia is now called _____ Iran.

18. _____ Dominican Republic is located in _____ Central America.

19. _____ Downing Street is a famous street in _____ London.

20. One slope of _____ Mt. Blanc is in _____ France, another in _____ Switzerland.

21. His parents were born in _____ Philippines.

THE WITH PLACE NAMES (2)
SPECIFIC RULES

Place Names with **The**	*Place Names without* **The**
Most bodies of water:	*Continents*:
the Mississippi River	Europe
the Pacific Ocean	Africa
the Mediterranean Sea	North America
the English Channel	*Countries*:
the Panama Canal	France, Peru, Japan
the Persian Gulf	*but* the Congo, the Sudan
but the Gulf of Mexico	*Cities, states*:
the Bering Strait	Hong Kong, Buenos Aires, London, California,
(*The word* Ocean, Sea *or* River	Florida
may be omitted—the Mississippi)	*but* the Hague, the Vatican
Mountain ranges:	*Lakes, bays*:
the Rocky Mountains (The word *Mountains* may	Lake Michigan
be omitted—the Rockies.)	Hudson Bay
No **the** *with one mountain*—Mount Everest, Bear	*but* the Bay of Biscay
Mountain	*Islands*:
Peninsulas:	Coney Island, Wake Island
the Scandinavian Peninsula	*but* the Philippine Islands (the word **Islands** may
Libraries, museums:	be omitted—the Philippines)
the Louvre	*Universities, colleges*:
the Metropolitan Museum	Columbia University
the Forty-Second St. Library	*but* the University of California
Points of the compass used as names for geographic	*Streets, avenues, boulevards*:
areas:	Pennsylvania Avenue
the South, the Middle West, the Near East	Forty-second Street
but Southern California	*Parks*:
Special points on the globe:	Hyde Park, Central Park
the North Pole	
the Equator	
the 42nd Parallel	
Hotels:	
the Statler Hotel	
the Carlyle Hotel	
(The word **Hotel** may be omitted.)	

Supply **the** wherever needed.

1. _____ Amazon is the largest river system in the world.

2. _____ North America is bounded on the east by
_____ Atlantic Ocean and on the west by _____
Pacific Ocean.

3. A few seas have the names of colors: _____ Black Sea,
_____ Red Sea, _____ Yellow
Sea.

4. _____ Suez Canal is in _____ Middle East.

5. _____ Mediterranean is a beautiful sea.

6. _____ Allegheny Mountains are in the eastern part of _____ North America.

7. _____ St. Petersburg is now called _____ Leningrad.

8. _____ Far East, or _____ Orient, refers to the area of _____ Asia where _____ China and _____ Japan are located.

9. He used to live in _____ South, but then he moved to _____ California.

10. _____ Balkan Peninsula is surrounded by _____ Black Sea and _____ Adriatic, Ionian and Aegean Seas of _____ Mediterranean.

11. _____ Russia and _____ Alaska almost meet at _____ Bering Strait.

12. _____ Brazil covers nearly half the continent of _____ South America.

13. _____ Norway and _____ Sweden occupy _____ Scandinavian Peninsula; _____ Portugal and _____ Spain comprise _____ Iberian Peninsula.

14. _____ Strait of Gibraltar separates _____ Europe from _____ Africa.

15. Tea is grown in many parts of _____ southern Asia, especially in _____ India and _____ Ceylon.

16. _____ British Museum houses an immense library.

17. _____ Louvre and _____ Metropolitan Museum are both world-famous.

18. _____ New York Stock Exchange is located on _____ Wall Street.

19. _____ Columbia University, _____ Princeton University, and _____ Yale University are all regarded as excellent American universities.

20. There are many beautiful shops on _____ Fifth Avenue in _____ New York.

21. _____ Central Park is right in the heart of _____ New York City.

22. _____ Royal Hawaiian Hotel is one of the oldest in _____ Honolulu.

23. _____ Istanbul was once called _____ Constantinople.

6-10

***THE* WITH WORDS
OF TIME AND PLACE**

Time

1. Points in a progression—**the beginning, the middle, the end**
2. Points in a time continuum—**the past, the present, the future**
3. Parts of the day—**in the morning, in the afternoon, in the evening** (*but* **at noon, at midnight**)
4. Seasons—**in the winter** (*or* **summer, autumn, spring**). **The** is sometimes omitted here, especially in a general statement—**In (the) winter we go skiing in the Alps.**
5. Time expressions meaning **this**—**at the** (= **this**) **moment, for the time being, during the year, all the while**

Place

> the top, the bottom, the middle
>
> the back, the front, the side, the center
>
> the inside (or interior), the outside (or exterior)

No article is used with nouns denoting certain places in the environment.

He is going to { church.
                  school, or elementary school, high school, but **the** university.
                  prison, or jail.

He is going { home.
               downtown.

Supply **the** where needed.

1. At _____ beginning, he couldn't get used to the food.

2. At _____ first, she didn't like her English teacher, but toward _____ middle of the semester she began to appreciate him.

3. Don't worry so much about _____ future; it's _____ present that is most important.

4. He takes his lunch at _____ noon.

5. In _____ middle of the road sat a puppy who would not budge at the sound of the horn.

6. The point the author was trying to make was stated at _____ beginning of the book.

7. _____ inside of the house was gaily decorated for the party. However there were no decorations _____ outside.

8. Many of the chief characters in the play die at _____ end.

9. She is taking several history courses at _____ present.

10. He is on the telephone at _____ present moment.

11. They went _____ downtown to do some shopping.

12. These flowers bloom in _____ spring.

13. Her youngest son is now going to _____ high school.

14. He can't fall asleep at _____ night if there is any noise.

15. During _____ night there was a great deal of noise outside our window.

6-11
THE WITH WORDS
REFERRING TO EVENTS, GOVERNMENT

1. Names of historical periods or events—**the Ming Dynasty, the Middle Ages, the Renaissance, the French Revolution, the Civil War, the First World War** (but **World War II**).
2. Names of bills, acts, and other legislative deliberations—**the Magna Carta, the Taft-Hartley Bill, the Missouri Compromise.**
3. Official titles—**the Secretary of State, the Foreign** (or **Prime**) **Minister, the King, the Premier,** (but no *the* if the name accompanies the title—**President Washington**).
4. Law enforcement bodies, civil and military—**the Army, the Navy, the Air Corps, the state militia, the police, the highway patrol.**
5. Names of branches of the government—**the executive** (or the **legislative**, the **judicial**) **branch.**
6. Names of institutions, foundations, organizations—**the United Nations, the Ford Foundation, the Girl Scouts.**
7. Names of political parties—**the Labor party, the Conservative party, the Democratic party, the Communist party. The** name of the party is often used in the plural without the word **party—the Democrats, the Republicans, the Conservatives.**

Articles are generally not used with names of holidays—**Thanksgiving, Christmas, Easter,** but—**the Fourth of July.**

Supply **the** where needed.

1. Da Vinci painted during _____ Italian Renaissance.

2. _____ World War Two ended in 1945.

3. _____ Industrial Revolution brought about great changes in western civilization.

4. _____ American Constitution guarantees freedom of speech.

5. _____ President of the United States and _____ _____ Prime Minister of England are both heads of state.

6. _____ Parliament is not in session today.

7. _____ Navy reported the loss of two ships.

8. _____ police are holding two men on suspicion of murder.

9. _____ Thanksgiving is celebrated at the end of November.

10. _____ legislative branch of the government makes the laws; _____ executive branch carries them out.

11. He belongs to _____ Democratic party.

12. _____ President Nixon made many speeches in _____ Congress.

13. _____ Supreme Court is going to announce their decision on this case soon.

14. _____ Monroe Doctrine stated that European countries were not to interfere in the affairs of Latin America.

15. _____ Election Day occurs on the Tuesday after the first Monday in November.

6-12
THE IN *OF* PHRASES
AFTER WORDS EXPRESSING QUANTITY

A determiner is required in an **of** phrase after a word of indefinite quantity or after a numeral. This determiner is usually **the**.

Most
All
Many
One-third   } of **the** students (in this class) passed the examination.
Five
The majority

Many of these words expressing quantity may also be followed by nouns without **of the**.

Most
Many   } students (in this class) passed the examination.
Five

Supply **the** where needed.

EXAMPLE: a. Many of _____ the _____ men in the room were protesting against the new regulations.

  b. Many _____ — _____ men died in the war.

1. Most _____ clerical mistakes are the result of carelessness.

2. Most of _____ clerical mistakes in our office could be avoided if the clerks paid more attention to their work.

3. Some _____ students are lazy.

4. Some of _____ students I know are lazy.

5. Both of _____ men who were charged with disorderly conduct were fined by the judge.

6. Both _____ men disobeyed the law.

7. Many _____ arguments have been presented for equality for all before the law.

8. Many of _____ arguments presented for equality were very powerful.

9. All _____ men are created equal.

10. All of _____ men who have been accused will be given a fair trial.

11. Very few _____ men would be as patient with a nagging wife as he is.

12. Very few of _____ men returned from their air raid mission.

13. Four _____ passengers were hurt in the accident.

14. Four of _____ passengers in the car were hurt in the accident.

6-13
THE IN CONSTRUCTIONS LIKE *THE MORE, THE MERRIER*

This older type of construction is still in common use today. **The** may appear adverbially with single words or with whole clauses.

> *The* more, *the* merrier.
> *The* harder he works, *the* less he succeeds.
> *The* prettier the girl (is), *the* more foolishly he behaves.

Change each sentence into a **the . . . the** construction.

EXAMPLE: a. If the challenge is great, he likes it more.
  The greater the challenge (is), the more he likes it. _____

  b. As they argued, they became angrier.
  The more they argued, the angrier they became. _____

1. If he spends less money now, he'll have more later.

_____

2. If he comes sooner, this will be better. (Use only **the better** in the second part.)

_____

3. If his clothes are shabby, he likes them better.

_____

4. If we get to the theater later, we'll get worse seats.

_____

5. If a restaurant is large, its service is more impersonal.

_____

6. If we do more work now, we'll have less to do later.

_____

7. If you take less baggage, you'll be better off.

_____

8. If you say less to him about the matter, this will be better.

_____

9. As he worked longer, his job became easier.

_____

10. As he sees her more, he likes her more.

_____

11. As he grew older, he became more eccentric.

_____

12. As she did more for him, he complained more.

_____

13. As she cooks more, she becomes better.

_____

14. As he learns more about life, he becomes more cynical.

_____

15. As prices rose higher, the workers asked for more money.

_____

16. As he earned more money, he spent more.

_____

6-14
INDEFINITE *A* vs. INDEFINITE *SOME*

Corresponding to indefinite **a** used with singular countable nouns is indefinite **some** used with plural nouns or with noncountable nouns.

I need	a	chair.
I need	some	chairs.
I need	some	furniture.

In such indefinite use, it is possible to omit **some** but not **a**.

A. Use **a** or **some**.

EXAMPLE: a. She wants _____ some _____ stationery. (noncountable noun)

b. She wants _____ some _____ pencils. (plural noun)

c. She wants _____ a _____ pencil. (singular countable noun)

1. They are building _____ new house.

2. Isn't tomorrow _____ holiday?

3. Please give me _____ information about this university.

4. I would like _____ toast and _____ _____ cup of coffee.

5. They are planning to buy _____ expensive camera.

6. _____ children were playing in the school yard when _____ explosion was heard.

7. I need _____ hammer and _____ nails.

8. She has just bought _____ new clothes.

9. Can you lend me _____ pair of scissors?

B. Change the italicized nouns to singular form. Change the verbs or modifiers if necessary.

EXAMPLE: a. They were watching some *geese* in the pond.
They were watching a goose in the pond.

b. Some *churches* are being built in this area.
A church is being built in this area.

1. Please put some steak *knives* on the table.

_____

2. She put some *coins* in the washing machine.

_____

3. He is having some *teeth* extracted.

_____

4. At the zoo the children saw some *monkeys* jumping from limb to limb.

_____

5. Some *thieves* broke into their apartment.

_____

6. You'll find some *tomatoes* in the refrigerator.

_____

7. Some *cargoes* of bananas are being unloaded now.

_____

8. The woman got frightened because she saw some *mice* in the basement.

_____

9. Some *sheep* were grazing in the field.

_____

10. Some *alumni* of the college were financing the new gymnasium.

_____

11. The prime minister had to cut his vacation short because some *crises* had arisen in the government.

_____

6-15
INDEFINITE *A* vs. CLASSIFYING *A*

Indefinite **a** and classifying **a** may be distinguished from each other by their different plurals.

	Singular	*Plural*
Indefinite **a**	*He ate **an** apple.*	*He ate **some** apples.*
Classifying **a**	*He is **a** good student.*	*They are good students.*
	A lion is very strong.	*Lions are very strong.*

Note that **some** is used with the plural of indefinite **a**, but not with the plural of classifying **a**.

Change the following sentences by using the plural of the italicized words. Make whatever other changes are necessary.

EXAMPLE: a. A *student* was writing on the blackboard.
Some students were writing on the blackboard.

b. A *horse* is an *animal*.
Horses are animals.

1. He was excited about a beautiful *bird* he had just seen.

_____

2. There is a *river* in this region.

_____

3. A *river* is a *body of water*.

_____

4. He is writing a long *article* about water pollution.

_____

5. This recipe requires an *egg*.

_____

6. An *egg* should be eaten fresh.

_____

7. We received an important *letter* yesterday.

_____

8. An *applicant* for the job was waiting to be interviewed.

_____

9. *He* is a corporation *lawyer*.

_____

10. A *demagogue* tries to gain political power by playing on people's emotions.

_____

11. *She* is a hard-working *nurse*.

_____

12. A *pigeon* flew into the room.

_____

13. A *horse* has a *mane* and a *tail*.

_____

14. A *monarchy* is ruled by a *king* or a *queen*.

_____

15. A *carrot* is a yellow vegetable.

_____

16. *He* is a *man* who knows what he wants.

_____

17. A *patient* was transferred to another ward of the hospital.

_____

6-16
CLASSIFYING A

A. Use a sentence placing each word in the smaller class into one of the words in the larger class. Use the dictionary if necessary.

Smaller class	*Larger class*
1. monkey	bird
2. lettuce	flower
3. bee	continent
4. bronze	gas
5. lily	kind of wine
6. nitrogen	animal
7. Africa	car
8. Cadillac	industry
9. newspaper	insect
10. parrot	article of clothing
11. champagne	metal
12. belt	vegetable
13. coal mining	medium of communication

EXAMPLE: a. A monkey is an animal. _____

b. Lettuce is a vegetable. _____

B. Note which words in the smaller class can also be used with **the** (usually names of species of insects, birds, plants, animals).

C. Change all the sentences from A. into the plural, if possible.

EXAMPLE: a. Monkeys are animals. _____

b. no change possible with noncountable **lettuce.** _____

6-17
WHAT (A), SUCH (A)

What a and **such a** occur only with singular countable nouns, not with plural or noncountable nouns.

Change into sentences with **what** and **such**.

EXAMPLE: a. Mary, is, pretty girl. (singular countable noun)
What a pretty girl Mary is. _____
Mary is such a pretty girl. _____

b. They, are, pretty girls. (plural countable noun)
What pretty girls they are. _____
They are such pretty girls. _____

c. Mary, has, pretty hair. (noncountable noun)
What pretty hair Mary has. _____
Mary has such pretty hair. _____

1. She, is, good cook.

_____

_____

2. The child, has, lovely eyes.

_____

_____

3. She, has, expensive furniture.

_____

_____

4. This, is, big house.

_____

_____

5. We, are having, fine weather.

_____

_____

6. This, is, hot climate.

_____

_____

7. It, is, cold day.

_____

_____

8. They, are gathering, useless information.

_____

_____

9. This car, has, powerful motor.

_____

_____

10. She, has, long eyelashes.

_____

_____

11. They, are, helpless people.

_____

_____

12. We, saw, beautiful rainbow.

_____

_____

13. You, have on, chic dress.

_____

_____

14. This, is, fancy restaurant.

_____

_____

15. She, has, good taste.

_____

_____

16. He, has made, ambiguous statement.

_____

_____

17. We, are all, having, good time.

_____

_____

18. He, has had, hard life.

_____

_____

19. She, has, forgetful nature.

_____

_____

20. He, made, rude remark.

_____

_____

21. The children, are wearing, dirty clothes.

_____

_____

22. This, is, tasteless food.

_____

_____

6-18
A WITH NOUNS THAT ARE
BOTH COUNTABLE AND NONCOUNTABLE

Some nouns that are derived from verbs may have both a countable and a noncountable use. The noncountable word refers to the act itself—**operation, mixture, shipment, government**—and the countable word to the concrete product or the result of the act—**an imitation, a shipment, a government**.

The child learns through imitation.

but { Art is an imitation of life.
This picture is a good imitation.

Supply the article **a** wherever it indicates the concrete product or the result of an act.

EXAMPLE: a. The electric light was _____ an _____ important invention.

b. _____ — _____ necessity is the mother of _____ — _____ invention.

1. He is _____ authority on ancient Greece.

2. That painting is _____ possession he dearly prizes.

3. For the hedonist, _____ pleasure is considered the greatest good.

4. Meeting you has been _____ great pleasure.

5. We will ship out the merchandise on _____ receipt of your order.

6. His landlord always gives him _____ receipt for the rent.

7. _____ growth and _____ maturation are important processes of _____ life.

8. He is living _____ life of ease.

9. Everyone would like to be free from _____ pain.

10. She told the doctor she had _____ pain in her back.

11. _____ variety is the spice of _____ life.

12. The salesman showed her _____ variety of shoes.

13. The Stoics felt we should calmly accept our fate without expressing _____ grief or _____ joy.

14. She checked with the doctor about _____ tiny growth on her chin.

15. _____ revolution is going on right now in that country.

16. The doctor told him he might need _____ operation on his leg.

17. Everyone who admires _____ democracy would like to live in _____ democracy.

6-19
A WITH NONCOUNTABLE NOUNS

In some sentences, noncountable abstract nouns *with adjective modifiers* may be used with **a**. In many such sentences **a** is the equivalent of *a kind of*.

He exhibited *a* courage *that surprised me*.

We encountered *an unexpected* friendliness wherever we went.

Use **a** or **the** with the abstract nouns.

EXAMPLE: a. He displayed _____ a _____ wisdom far beyond his years.

b. _____ The _____ wisdom he displayed was far beyond his years.

1. He has _____ simplicity which is seldom met with these days.

2. They live in _____ atmosphere of never-ceasing anxiety.

3. _____ atmosphere he creates in his novels is of never-ceasing anxiety.

4. He has _____ aversion for any kind of work.

5. _____ aversion he felt for any kind of work was unbelievable.

6. She enjoys _____ popularity which is well deserved.

7. He never told anyone about _____ loneliness he had experienced in the big city.

8. In the big city, he experienced _____ loneliness which he had never known before.

9. _____ knowledge of history gives us _____ sense of perspective.

10. The young man was seeking _____ independence which he could not find at home.

11. _____ profound distrust of his fellow men led him to become a recluse.

12. He felt _____ awareness of _____ hopelessness of his situation.

13. _____ better understanding of the problem will help us to solve it.

14. Everyone was impressed by _____ sincerity with which he spoke.

15. She has never forgotten _____ advice she received from her father.

16. He has had _____ excellent education in one of the best universities.

6-20
ARTICLES IN IDIOMS WITH VERBS

Some verbs form idioms with their objects. Sometimes **a** is used with the object, sometimes **the**, and sometimes no article at all.

1. *A* with the object—**do a favor, tell a lie, make a living, make a remark, take a trip, take a picture, become a reality, play a joke on, call a halt, take a look at, make a mistake**

2. *The* with the object—**make the beds, clear the table, wash the dishes, tell the truth**

3. *No article* with the object—**make friends with, take care of, take revenge on, shake hands, take pride in, take part in, take notice of, have faith in, take pity on, take advantage of, make fun of.**

Use **a, the,** or leave blank.

1. He made _____ mistake in his addition.

2. Space travel has now become _____ reality.

3. He makes _____ friends with people very easily.

4. He often makes _____ fun of people or takes _____ advantage of them.

5. We should always try to tell _____ truth, but sometimes it is better to tell _____ little lie.

6. He makes _____ living by writing books.

7. She has taken _____ part in many amateur theatrical productions.

8. When he took _____ trip to India, he took _____ picture of the Taj Mahal.

9. He takes _____ pride in his country and has _____ faith in it.

10. I must clear _____ table and wash _____ dishes before we can go out.

11. Let's call _____ halt to this bitter argument and shake _____ hands.

12. Would you do me _____ favor and make _____ beds for me?

13. The close observation of other planets is now becoming _____ reality.

14. The company takes _____ care of all the traveling expenses of its salesmen.

7

Adverbs

STRUCTURAL DESCRIPTION OF ADVERBS

Types of Adverbs and Function	Position of Adverbs	Form of Adverbs

1. *Manner*—modifies the verb
quickly
awkwardly
2. *Place and direction*—modifies the verb
here, away, outside, left, straight, west
3. *Time*—modifies the verb
  a. definite
    today
    yesterday
    tomorrow
  b. indefinite
    recently
    later
    always
4. *Intensifying*
  a. degree—modifies an adjective or adverb
    very (strong)
    quite (frequently)
  b. emphasizing—modifies all parts of speech
    even (she)
    only (once)
5. *Conjunctive adverb*—modifies the sentence
therefore
nevertheless
6. *Sentence adverb*—modifies the sentence
    fortunately
    actually
	1. *Initial position*
	Sometimes she comes late.
	(position of greatest emphasis)
	2. *Mid-position* (with verb)
	She sometimes comes late.
	3. *Final position*
	She comes late sometimes.
		1. *Grammatical* (for comparison)
		  a. *more . . . than*
		    more quickly than
		    the most . . .
		    the most quickly
		  b. **. . . -er than** (for short adverbs often having the same form as adjectives)
		    faster than
		    the . . . -est
		    the fastest
		2. *Derivational*
		Mostly **-ly** added to adjectives
		quickly
		extremely
		Two or more words may combine to form an adverbial word group—**so far, the day before yesterday, as a matter of fact.**
		
		Markers of Adverbs
		Degree intensifiers
		  very, quite, etc.

POSITION OF ADVERBIALS

Although it is possible for an adverb or an adverbial word group to occupy initial position, mid-position with the verb, or final position, all three positions are not always possible for each type of adverb. The more common positions for the different types of adverbs are as follows.

Adverbs of manner	*final position* *but also*: mid-position initial position	She dances very **gracefully**. She **quickly** left the room. **Quickly**, he took out his gun and fired.
Adverbs of place and direction	*final position* *but also*: initial position	It's cold **outside**. **Outside**, it was bitterly cold.
Adverbs of time definite indefinite	*final position* *but also*: initial position *mid-position* *but also*: initial position final position	The ship will arrive **tomorrow**. **Tomorrow**, we will leave for Chicago. They were **recently** married. **Recently**, the news about the nation's economy has not been good. We have been having many strikes **recently**.
Conjunctive adverbs	*initial position* *or* *mid-position* *but also*: final position	The motor you sent is defective; **therefore**, we are returning it to you. . . .; we are **therefore** returning it to you. . . .; we are returning it to you **therefore**.
Sentence adverbs	*initial position* *but also*: mid-position final position	Two cars collided at that intersection; **fortunately**, no one was hurt. . . .; no one, **fortunately**, was hurt. . . .; no one was hurt, **fortunately**.

Intensifiers appear directly before the words they modify—**It is very** (or **quite, rather, extremely**) **cold outside.**

Commas used with adverbials are often optional; such commas usually represent a pause in speech.

Place the adverbials in parentheses in the most usual position. Note other possible positions for these adverbials. Keep in mind that initial position is the position of greatest emphasis.

1. (quietly) The nurse moved from one patient to another.

_____

2. (mysteriously) One of his valuable paintings disappeared.

_____

3. (very rudely) He spoke to her.

_____

4. (outside) There are some people waiting.

_____

5. (over there) Put those packages.

_____

6. (ten years ago) There were only private homes in this neighborhood.

_____

7. (in a few years) We may be able to send a man to Mars.

_____

8. (today) (on the doorstep) The milkman didn't put any milk.

_____

9. (recently) There have been many floods.

_____

10. (now) Let's not do the dishes. (later) We can do them.

_____

11. (never) We have had trouble with this car.

_____

12. (for a long time) I haven't seen him.

_____

13. (always) He has been working for the government.

_____

14. (quite) The boy is insolent to his mother.

_____

15. (nearly) The work is finished.

_____

16. (especially) She's not pretty.

_____

17. (obviously) He doesn't want to lose any money in this business deal.

_____

18. (certainly) They will refund your deposit if you decide not to go on the tour.

_____

19. (definitely) I saw someone hiding behind those bushes.

---

20. He didn't feel he had a chance to be accepted by one of the large universities; (therefore) he decided to apply to the small college near his home.

7-2

ADVERBS IN MID-POSITION (WITH THE VERB)

The position of an adverb with the verb varies according to the number of auxiliaries that accompany the verb.

	Usual Position of Adverb	*Sentences*

1. *Verbs with no auxiliaries* (Simple present and simple past tenses)
   a. *the verb* **be**
   b. *all other verbs*
	after the verb
	before the verb
		She is **sometimes** late.
		She **sometimes** comes late.

2. *Verbs with one to three auxiliaries*	*after the first auxiliary*	She has **sometimes** come late. She has **sometimes** been coming late.

A less usual position for an adverb in mid-position is before the independent verb **be** or the first auxiliary.

> She sometimes is late.
> She sometimes has come late.
> She sometimes has been coming late.

An important rule to remember about an adverb in mid-position is that it is generally not placed between the verb and its object.[1]

Place the adverb in parentheses in *the most usual position* with the verb. Be careful not to place an adverb between a verb and its object.

1. (soon) He will be on his way to fame and fortune.

---

2. (frequently) They were absent from school.

---

[1] However, an adverb of manner may appear before a long object—**Please read carefully all the sections in the book that deal with adverbs.**

3. (usually) He is calm and even-tempered.

_____

4. (later) He regretted having made a promise he couldn't keep.

_____

5. (almost never) She loses her temper.

_____

6. (seldom) She leaves the children unattended.

_____

7. (usually) This disease is fatal; (seldom) patients recover from it.

_____

8. (first) The robber made sure that no one was looking before (stealthily) he crept through the window.

_____

9. (systematically) The retreating army blew up all the bridges behind them.

_____

10. (always) They have expressed the same opinion about everything.

_____

11. (now) They have completed the foundation for the building.

_____

12. (completely) He has misunderstood what I have been saying.

_____

13. (surely) They have arrived by now.

_____

14. (probably) He will take the dog to the veterinarian today.

_____

15. (utterly) Their house was ruined by the flood.

_____

16. (evidently) She has been interfering in all her son's affairs.

_____

17. (recently) He has been invited to give a talk on data processing.

_____

7-3
TWO ADVERBS IN MID-POSITION

Two adverbs may be used in mid-position.

> They are **now rapidly** approaching retirement age. (verb with one auxiliary)
> He will **surely** be **severely** punished. (verb with two auxiliaries)

The second adverb, which is usually an adverb of manner, is placed closest to the main part of the verb.

Insert the adverbs in parentheses in mid-position with the verb. In some sentences the first adverb may have more than one position. Be careful not to put an adverb between the verb and its object.

1. (soon, amply) You will be rewarded for your help.

_____

2. (now, completely) These generals have undermined the confidence of the people in the government.

_____

3. (already, sharply) They have reduced the prices of all their merchandise.

_____

4. (severely, soon) Their activities will be curtailed on account of the curfew.

_____

5. (usually, thoroughly) They have been convinced that they were right before they took any action.

_____

_____

6. (exquisitely, always) She is dressed at these affairs.

_____

7. (really, thoroughly) He should be reprimanded for his laxness on the job.

_____

8. (obviously, really) He intends to carry out his threat.

_____

9. (falsely, actually) The servant was accused of stealing the jewelry.

_____

10. He jumped forward when he heard the noise behind him. (thus, narrowly) He escaped injury.

_____

_____

11. (always, absolutely) He is sure of victory.

_____

12. (light-heartedly, soon) He will be sailing away on his yacht.

_____

13. (securely, now) They are tying down the lawn chairs so that the wind won't blow them away.

_____

_____

7-4
ADVERBIALS IN FINAL POSITION

An adverb or adverbial word group used in final position appears after the verb and any complement(s) it may have. If more than one adverbial occurs in final position, the usual order is *place, manner, time.*

1 Subject	2 Verb + Complement	3 Place	4 Manner also: *Instrument, Agent,* *Accompaniment, Degree,* *Purpose*	5 Frequency	6 Other Kinds of Time
I	appreciate him		more and more (*degree*)		each time I see him.
She	cut the bread		slowly (*manner*) with a dull knife. (*instrument*)		
He	was walking	along the street	quietly (*manner*) with his dog (*accompaniment*)		last night.
We	hope to go	to Hawaii	for a vacation (*purpose*)		next month.
This toy	may be made	at home	by young people (*agent*) very easily (*manner*) with a few simple tools. (*instrument*)		
They	put the box	in a dry place	for safe keeping (*purpose*)		during the storm.
Mr. Lee	visited his wife	in the hospital		every day	for a month last year.

Actually, there is some degree of flexibility in the sequence of adverbials in final position. A general rule seems to be that a shorter adverbial precedes a longer one. However, a one-word adverbial of place like **here, there, away,** usually remains closest to the verb, and an adverbial of definite time like **today, yesterday** generally comes last.

Adverbials expressing *purpose*, especially infinitives, often follow other adverbials in final position—**We'll call a meeting next week to discuss his proposal.**

Arrange each of the following so that all adverbials are in final position. In some sentences there may be more than one acceptable arrangement of adverbials.

EXAMPLE: at all times, a guard, there, is, in the building.
There is a guard in the building at all times.

1. on the line, the clothes, hangs, she, early in the morning.

2. at the same cafeteria, eat, at exactly the same time, they, every day.

3. he, to the post office, to mail the letters, at 5:00 P.M., his office boy, sent.

4. very enthusiastically, the last time I saw him, spoke, he, about the new play.

5. hastily, while he was waiting for her, something, wrote, he, on a piece of paper.

6. after the trial, the lawyer, everyone, highly, commended.

7. hesitantly, walked, the defendant, into the courtroom.

8. several times, around the block, he, before he found a parking space, drove.

9. impatiently, waited, for the play to begin, they.

10. overtime, so that he can pay for his new car, has been working, he.

11. intermittently, was exchanged, across the border, all through the night, gunfire.

12. for three hours, must simmer, the stew, slowly.

13. into their new house, the day before yesterday, moved, they.

14. to Hong Kong, he, is going, to buy some jade, with his wife.

_____

15. the flowers, in the garden, by his wife, were planted, last spring.

_____

7-5

DISTRIBUTION OF ADVERBIALS

When several adverbials are used in a sentence, the tendency is to distribute them among the various positions that are natural for them—***Every day** he *eagerly* checked the stock market reports *to see if his stocks had gone up.***

Arrange the adverbials in each of the following in the best possible way. (Some adverbials may work equally well in two positions.) Use commas where you would pause in speech, keeping in mind that a long introductory adverbial is likely to be cut off with a comma.

EXAMPLE: has been, extremely, ever since his accident, he, about his driving, careful.

Ever since his accident, he has been extremely careful about his driving.

(Ever since his accident may also appear at the end.)

1. lately, heavy, she, rather, has become.

_____

2. I, last night, was, tired, quite, after a hard day at the office.

_____

_____

3. before you come to dinner, your hands, away, put, quickly, your toys, and wash.

_____

_____

4. the patient, ate, for the first time, eagerly, today, all the food on his tray.

_____

_____

5. the students, slowly, at the signal, down the aisle, marched, in single file.

_____

_____

6. always, of others who are worse off than you, think, when you are feeling depressed.

_____

_____

7. for the first time in two days, to clear away the snow, outside, they, were able to go.

_____

_____

8. near the window, the students, every day, for ten minutes, to do deep-breathing exercises, stand.

_____

_____

9. by secret agents, wherever she went, she was watched, for a long time, closely.

_____

_____

10. put, in the oven, right away, the cookies.

_____

_____

7-6
REVERSAL OF WORDS ORDER
AFTER CERTAIN ADVERBIALS

The subject and verb are often reversed after initial (1) negatives (or near negatives), (2) **only, so** or **such**, (3) expressions of place. Such a reversal, which permits more emphasis to be placed on the adverbial in initial position, often represents formal usage.

Reversal
After Initial Negatives
(or Near Negatives)

Never	have	I	seen	such a sight.
Seldom	did	they	have	enough to eat.
No sooner	had	he	left	the office than he received an important telephone call.

The negative conjunctions **not only**, **nor**, **neither** also require such reversals.

Not only is his new car less expensive then the old one, but it also uses less gasoline.
She doesn't know where her former husband is living, nor does she care to know.

Move the italicized negative or near-negative elements to the beginning of the sentence. Be sure to reverse the order of subject and verb.

EXAMPLE: a. He had *never* been allowed to do as he pleased.
Never had he been allowed to do as he pleased.

b. There has been *no* complete justice *at any time in history*.
At no time in history has there been complete justice.

1. You will *never again* have another opportunity like this.

_____

2. He did *not* complain *once* about his financial difficulties.

_____

3. He had *scarcely* entered the room when he was greeted by the host and hostess.

_____

_____

4. He *never* failed to bring his wife a gift for her birthday.

_____

5. He has *not, on any occasion,* disregarded the rights of the workers. (Use *on no occasion.*)

_____

_____

6. Such a solution has *seldom* worked in the past.

_____

7. I will *never again* lend him any money.

_____

8. There will *seldom* be any need for such an extreme measure.

_____

9. I would *never in the world* care to go through that terrible experience again.

_____

_____

10. The factory *not only* had a burglar alarm system, but it had a watchman patrolling the grounds day and night.

_____

_____

11. This door is *not* to be unlocked *at any time.* (Use *at no time.*)

_____

12. They have never traveled to a foreign country. They do *not* expect to do so in the future. (Begin the second sentence with *nor.*)

_____

_____

Reversal After
Initial ONLY, SO or SUCH

Only once	did	she	complain about the amount of work she had to do.
So extensive	was	the damage	that the house had to be completely rebuilt.
Such a powerful man	was	he	that no one dared to oppose him.

Move the italicized words to the beginning of the sentence. Make the necessary reversal of subject and verb.

EXAMPLE: a. We get a chance to go camping *only once in a while*.
Only once in a while do we get a chance to go camping.

b. She entered the room *so silently* that no one noticed her.
So silently did she enter the room that no one noticed her.

c. He realized how much she meant to him *only when he had lost her*.
Only when he had lost her did he realize how much she meant to him.

1. This exit is to be used *only in the event of fire*.

_____

2. I will consent to see him *only if he apologizes*.

_____

3. He realized what a tremendous task he had accomplished *only after the mural was completed*.

_____

_____

4. An exception can be made *only in rare cases*.

_____

5. The artist did *not* permit anyone *even once* to enter his studio.

_____

6. His answers were *so circumspect* that no useful information could be learned from them.

_____

_____

7. They were *such rare birds* that they had not even been recorded in any book.

_____

_____

8. The fire spread *so rapidly* that it took many days to get it under control.

_____

_____

Reversal
After Initial Expressions
of Place

There	stood	the tallest man he had ever seen.
Before them	lay	a vast expanse of desert.
Inside the room	were	a few dilapidated pieces of furniture.
Among those present	were	the governor and his wife.

Such reversals often occur with the verbs **be, stand, lie, sit**, but may also occur with other verbs. The auxiliary **do** is not used in reversals after place; also the parts of a passive verb are not separated—**In the box** *was found* **a large sum of money.**

Not all initial adverbials of place require a reversal of subject and verb—**In his hand he held a small round object.**

Move the italicized adverbials of place to the beginning of the sentence. Make the necessary reversal of subject and verb.

EXAMPLE: A large, shiny object lay *on the ground.*
      On the ground lay a large, shiny object.

1. The person who has committed the murder is *here, in this very room.*

2. Some of the most prominent citizens of the town were *among those collaborating with the army of occupation.*

3. There was a beautiful waterfall *at the end of the trail.* (omit *there*)

4. The little store where I buy my groceries is *around the corner.*

5. You will see such beautiful flowers *nowhere else.*

6. Books, magazines, newspapers were piled *on the desk.*

7. Many varieties of mushrooms can be found *in these woods.*

8. The peak of the great mountain loomed *far off in the distance.*

9. The decisive battle of the war was fought *on this very ground.*

10. A small child who asked for food appeared *seemingly out of nowhere.*

_____

11. A large tatoo of an eagle was *on his left arm.*

_____

-*LY* ADVERBS (1)

Adverbs of manner are formed by adding **-ly** to adjectives. When changing adjectives to adverbs, keep in mind that:

1. final **y** becomes **i** before **-ly**—**happily, merrily** (but **gayly** or **gaily**)
2. final **e** is kept before **-ly**—**fortunately, sincerely** (but **wholly, truly**)
3. **le** preceded by a consonant is dropped before **-ly**—**simply, idly**
4. both **-ic** and **-ical** become **-ically**—**basically, geographically** (but **publicly**)

Change the following adjectives to -*ly* adverbs. Make whatever spelling changes are necessary.

busy _____	possible _____
accidental _____	potential _____
cheerful _____	true _____
cruel _____	occasional _____
efficient _____	hygienic _____
sensible _____	evident _____
excessive _____	public _____
favorable _____	simple _____
fierce _____	dry _____
sincere _____	total _____
extreme _____	historic _____
mechanical _____	skillful _____
whole _____	humble _____
full _____	hasty _____

customary _____   useful _____

equal _____   hopeless _____

incidental _____   unfortunate _____

necessary _____   systematic _____

7-8
-*LY* ADVERBS (2)

Change each sentence so that the adjective becomes an **-ly** adverb of manner.

EXAMPLE: a. She always dresses in a simple manner.
   She always dresses simply. _____

   b. She is a careless typist.
   She types carelessly. _____

   c. He gave a prompt answer.
   He answered promptly. _____

1. She walks in an awkward manner.

_____

2. He is a brave fighter.

_____

3. The audience applauded in an enthusiastic manner.

_____

4. He was treated in a cruel way.

_____

5. She is a shameless liar.

_____

6. He spoke in a modest but convincing manner.

_____

7. She replied in an angry manner.

_____

8. The boy gave a faithful promise that he would be home before midnight.

_____

9. He addressed the professor in a respectful manner.

_____

10. She is a graceful dancer.

_____

11. He expressed his views in a simple and sincere manner.

_____

12. The money was divided in an equal manner among all the children.

_____

13. He is a careful driver.

_____

14. He did the job in a systematic manner.

_____

15. This can be done in an easy way.

_____

7-9
ADVERBS vs. ADJECTIVES

With certain verbs, adjective forms may be used rather than adverbs. These adjective forms express a state rather than manner. Verbs taking adjectives are the linking verbs like **be, seem, look, appear, become.** In addition, a number of transitive verbs combine with adjectives to form idiomatic expressions—**grow worse, prove wrong, blow open, break loose, play fair, open wide, hold tight.**

Use the proper form of the word in parentheses.

EXAMPLE: a. That man looks (desperate).
> That man looks desperate.
_____

b. He was looking (desperate) for the wallet he had lost.
> He was looking desperately for the wallet he had lost.
_____

1. These eggs seem (fresh).

_____

2. This coffee was (fresh) made.

_____

3. The baby's skin feels very (smooth).

_____

4. I don't feel (good) today. My head hurts.[2]

_____

5. I feel (bad) about his losing his job.[2]

_____

6. He was (bad) hurt in the accident.

_____

7. He appears (uneasy) about something.

_____

8. He looked about him (uneasy).

_____

9. They don't play (fair).

_____

10. Do you think he was treated (fair)?

_____

11. I wonder what could have gone (wrong)?

_____

12. He was (wrong) accused of the murder.

_____

13. He held his head (high) even after defeat.

_____

14. He is (high) regarded in the community.

_____

15. This product is (cheap) made.

_____

16. The dentist asked his patient to open his mouth (wide).

_____

17. The lion broke (loose) from his cage.

_____

18. He becomes very (angry) when he doesn't get his way.

_____

[2]After the verb **feel, well** refers to one's physical health, **good** and **bad** to one's emotional state. (formal usage)

19. The rumor about their divorce proved (false).

_____

20. The machine was repaired yesterday. It is now working (good).

_____

21. The milk tastes (sour).

_____

22. He is (firm) convinced that he is (right).

_____

23. I wish you wouldn't slam the door so (hard).[3]

_____

24. Please don't drive so (fast). The sign says, Drive (Slow).[3]

_____

25. He (slow) turned his head from side to side.

_____

[3]Some adverbs have the same form as adjectives—**hard, fast, slow** (only after certain verbs), **early, late.**

8

Prepositions

Prepositions

Function—A preposition connects a noun structure to some other word in the sentence. The nominal structure may be:

1. *a noun*—The jeweler showed the diamond ring to **his wife.**
2. *a pronoun*—The jeweler showed the diamond ring to **her.**
3. *a gerund phrase*—The jeweler did not object to **showing the diamond ring to her.**
4. *a noun clause*—The jeweler showed the diamond ring to **whoever might be a potential buyer.**

    Special functions of prepositional forms:

    1. *part of verb* (verb-preposition combinations)—**keep on** (= continue), **get up** (= awake), **go over** (= review)
    2. *adverb* (mostly place and direction):
    He went down. (Down is an adverb).
    He went down the stairs. (Down is a preposition.)
    Some prepositional forms are also used as conjunctions (mostly time):
    I will see you **after** dinner is served. **(After** is a conjunction.)
    I will see you **after** dinner. **(After** is a preposition.)

Position—A preposition usually appears before its noun object.

A preposition may appear in final position in:

1. *a question*—Which house does he live **in?**
2. *an adjective clause*—There is the house (which) he lives **in.**
3. *a noun clause*—I don't know which house he lives **in.**

Form—A preposition may be composed of one, two, or three parts.

1. *one part*—of, on, at, by, from
2. *two parts*—because of, according to, apart from, as for
3. *three parts*—by means of, with reference to, on account of, in regard to

Prepositional Phrases

Function—

1. *adverbial*—sit **under a tree,** leave **at nine o'clock**
2. *adjectival*—the subway **under the street,** the meeting **at nine o'clock**
3. *nominal (as a "prepositional object" of a verb)*—dispose **of the goods,** wait **for John**

Position—An adjectival prepositional phrase appears after the noun it modifies (the student **in the back row**).

A nominal phrase appears after a verb (listen **to your parents**). An adverbial phrase has three possible positions:

1. *initial*—**In spite of her handicap,** the blind girl did well in school.
2. *mid*—The blind girl, **in spite of her handicap,** did well in school.
3. *final*—The blind girl did well in school **in spite of her handicap.**

It is possible to have a sequence of prepositional phrases:

1. *adverbial*—The members met **in Paris on July 16.**
2. *adjectival*—The meeting of the members **in Paris on July 16.**

PREPOSITIONS OF TIME

1. One point in time—**on** (with *days*—may be omitted informally);
   at (with *noon, night, midnight*; with the *time of day*);
   in (with *other parts of the day*, with *months*, with *years*, with *seasons*).
2. Extended time—**since, for** (sometimes omitted informally), **by, from-to** (or **from-until**), **during, (with)in**.

Supply the required preposition of time.

1. They are getting married _____ Friday _____ _____ six o'clock _____ the evening.

2. Exactly _____ midnight we were awakened by the shrill sound of the air raid sirens.

3. The reception will be _____ Sunday _____ four _____ the afternoon.

4. Spring begins _____ March 21, summer _____ June 21, autumn _____ Sept. 22, and winter _____ December 22.

5. The last time I saw him was _____ the spring of 1966.

6. The event took place _____ August.

7. He came to this country _____ August 5, 1968.

8. He came to this country _____ 1968.

9. Daffodils usually bloom _____ late March.

10. World War Two lasted _____ 1939 _____ 1945.

11. They say that _____ the spring a young man's fancy fondly turns to thoughts of love.

12. He has not felt well _____ a long time, ever _____ his accident.

13. He has been away from home _____ two weeks.

14. They never go out _____ night _____ the week.

15. _____ the storm, all the lights were out _____ several hours.

16. We'll be ready to leave _____ an hour from now.

17. We'll have finished all the work _____ the time you get here.

18. He has been away from home _____ January 12.

19. _____ tomorrow, the worst of the storm should be over.

20. Recently he has been having trouble getting to sleep _____ night.

21. The temperature is below zero. _____ a few hours the pond should be frozen over.

8-2
PREPOSITIONS OF PLACE

1. The point itself—**in**, **inside** (for something contained), **on** (the surface), **at** (a general vicinity).
2. Higher than a point—**over** (generally), **above** (directly).
3. Lower than a point—**under** (generally), **underneath** (close under), **beneath**, **below** (directly).
4. Neighboring the point—**near**, **by**, **next to**, **between**, **among**, **opposite**.

Supply the required preposition of place.

1. I'll meet you _____ the Statler Hotel.

2. If you want to reach that shelf you'd better stand _____ a chair.

3. You will find some stamps _____ the middle drawer of the desk.

4. We are still living _____ Bedford Avenue. We used to live _____ 450 Bedford Avenue, but we now live _____ 631 Bedford Avenue.

5. This apartment is 10D; 11D is the apartment directly _____ us.

6. _____ the box were the earrings she thought she had lost.

7. Some of the most expensive stores _____ New York are _____ Fifth Avenue.

8. _____ the front page of a newspaper are the most important stories of the day.

9. Please play _____ the house. It's too cold outside.

10. When you are sitting _____ the table for dinner, don't put your elbows _____ the table.

11. There is no one _____ the world who can help me now.

12. The boy hid the money _____ a rock _____ the garden.

13. A subterranean river runs _____ the ground.

14. The tax office is _____ the second floor.

15. A submarine operates _____ the surface of the water.

16. We'll wait for you _____ the lobby of the hotel.

17. He saw a dollar bill lying _____ the sidewalk.

18. Turn left _____ the next intersection.

19. The pupils were busy writing some exercises _____ their desks.

20. They arrived _____ the United States last week.[1]

21. The plane arrived _____ the airport two hours late.[1]

---

[1]**Arrive in** is used for a larger geographical area such as a country. **Arrive at** is used for a smaller area such as a building, a station, an airport. With cities or towns, **arrive in** is far more common than **arrive at**.

PREPOSITIONAL OBJECTS

Some verbs take objects that are introduced by prepositions.

at	glance, laugh, look, marvel, rejoice, shudder, smile, stare
of	approve, beware, consist, despair, smell
of *or* **about**	boast, dream, speak, talk, think
for	call, hope, long, look, mourn, pray, wait, watch, wish

Supply the preposition required after each verb.

1. He kept glancing impatiently _____ his watch.

2. We should beware _____ those who flatter.

3. The room smells _____ paint.

4. The old man spoke _____ the hair-raising experiences he had had as a spy.

5. Listen! Do you hear someone calling _____ help?

6. Don't embarrass him by laughing _____ his mistakes in English.

7. Sometimes I despair _____ ever finishing this job.

8. Those people long _____ the day their country will be free again.

9. Don't stare _____ her; just look _____ her quickly.

10. We rejoice _____ his miraculous escape.

11. Water consists _____ hydrogen and oxygen.

12. Lately he has been thinking _____ her a great deal.

13. Everyone shuddered _____ the tale of terror he told.

14. Her parents disapprove _____ her staying out late at night.

15. I'll wait _____ you here.

16. He has always dreamed _____ going to England.

17. I can't find my ring. I've looked _____ it everywhere.

18. He's forever boasting _____ his brave exploits in the last war.

19. She mourned _____ her deceased husband for a long time.

20. We've always marveled _____ her ability to get along with all kinds of people.

21. I can't talk _____ things I don't understand.

to	allude, aspire, conform, consent, listen, object, point, reply, resort, respond, subscribe, yield
(up)on	count, decide, depend, feed, impose, insist, plan, reflect, rely
with	associate, consult, cope, deal, dispense, interfere, join, meddle, part, side, unite, vie
from	abstain, cease, deviate, differ, dissent, emerge, escape, flee, recover, retire, shrink

Supply the preposition required after each verb.

1. We're counting _____ you not to interfere _____ _____ the project.

2. He mentioned the subject once, but he has never alluded _____ _____ it again.

3. The sun was reflecting _____ his windshield and making it difficult to drive.

4. Let's dispense _____ all formalities and abstain _____ _____ taking sides in this dispute.

5. Some prisoners had escaped _____ prison and were fleeing _____ their pursuers.

6. Many young people today refuse to conform _____ society's regulations.

7. A severe fine was imposed _____ him for his improper behavior in the courtroom.

8. He expects to retire _____ his job in a few months.

9. At first her parents objected _____ the young man, but they finally consented _____ their marriage.

10. I insist _____ seeing him at once.

11. After years of imprisonment, he was finally reunited _____ his family.

12. He never seems to be listening _____ what people say to him.

13. He is so sensitive that he cannot cope _____ all his problems.

14. A situation arose which they had not planned _____.

15. When people are desperate, they may resort _____ violence.

16. He subscribed _____ many magazines.

17. The outcome of the experiment depends _____ several factors.

18. This new batch of cookies differs somewhat _____ the first one.

in	believe, confide, consist, deal, delight, end, engage, excel, indulge, participate, persevere, result, succeed
for *or* **against**	contend, declare, demonstrate, fight, strike, strive, vote
against	immunize, plot, rebel, struggle
into	transform, turn
over	reign, rule

Supply the preposition required after each verb.

1. He doesn't believe _____ anything at all.

2. The young people today are demonstrating _____ war and _____ peace.

3. Someone who plots _____ his own country is a traitor.

4. That dictator rules _____ the people with an iron hand.

5. She has always confided _____ her husband.

6. They have transformed that old house _____ an antique shop.

7. Which candidate are you voting _____?

8. He deals only _____ modern paintings.

9. Men have often had to fight _____ freedom.

10. Her line has been busy for a long time, but we've finally succeeded _____ reaching her.

11. The whole project ended _____ failure.

12. Vaccines are available to immunize people _____ many diseases.

13. He excels _____ all sports.

14. Her son never liked to participate _____ class discussions.

15. If you persevere _____ your studies you are bound to succeed.

16. We must continue to struggle _____ poverty.

8-4

VERBS WITH DIRECT OBJECTS AND PREPOSITIONAL OBJECTS

A verb may have both a direct object and a prepositional object.

She always needs to remind **her husband of his dental appointments**.

Only the direct object becomes the subject of the passive.

The store was robbed of $500 last night.
(*active*—Someone robbed **the store** of $500 last night).

SECOND OBJECT WITH:

of	accuse, convict, deprive, persuade, rob, suspect
of *or* **about**	advise, convince, remind, warn
about	ask, question
from	borrow, buy, collect, conceal, distinguish, hide, keep, protect, rescue, stop
on	base, inflict
with	burden, connect, entrust, help, provide
for	ask, blame, condemn, forgive, reprimand, reproach, substitute

Supply the required preposition.

1. The man accused his partner _____ cheating.

2. She suspects her husband _____ infidelity but she cannot prove it.

3. We'll have to borrow some money _____ the bank to pay for our new car.

4. She reproached her friend _____ not having told her sooner.

5. I don't wish to burden you _____ all my difficulties.

6. I forgot to ask the doctor _____ the medication I should take.

7. I cannot distinguish one twin _____ the other.

8. Motorcyclists are required to wear helmets to protect their heads _____ serious injury.

9. He cannot be persuaded _____ the truth of that statement.

10. It took a few days before they were able to rescue the men _____ the mine that had caved in.

11. He was convicted _____ a crime he had not committed.

12. Something is wrong; I'm convinced _____ it.

13. Money was collected _____ the employees to buy a gift for the girl who was getting married.

14. He has already been warned _____ the danger of lung cancer.

15. He was blamed _____ not taking the proper precautions against fire hazards.

16. Everyone who is connected _____ the arrested gambler is being questioned by the police.

17. Oleomargarine may be substituted _____ butter in this recipe.

18. The American Constitution guarantees that no one shall be deprived _____ life, liberty or the pursuit of happiness.

19. The punishment which was inflicted _____ him was too severe.

20. You must get a good lawyer to advise you _____ your rights in this matter.

INDIRECT OBJECTS WITH OR WITHOUT *TO*

Some indirect objects may be used alone before the direct object, or in a **to** phrase after the direct object.

> He sent his wife some flowers.
> or He sent some flowers to his wife.
> She gave the cashier the money.
> or She gave the money to the cashier.

Other indirect objects may be used only in a **to** phrase after the direct object.

> She explained the lesson to the class.
> He described his home town to us.
> The doctor recommended a heart specialist to his patient.

Wherever possible, change the **to** indirect object to the form without **to**.

EXAMPLE: a. She gave some food to the dog.
　　　　　　She gave the dog some food.

　　　　　　b. The university dedicated the new building to its former president.
　　　　　　(*no change possible*)

1. Please bring the newspaper to me.

_____

2. Let me describe the scene to you.

_____

3. The cashier will refund the money to you.

_____

4. He handed the money to the salesclerk.

_____

5. We plan to sell our collection of paintings to one person only.[2]

_____

6. We plan to sell our house to them.

_____

7. You must explain all this to the judge.

_____

[2]A long indirect object is not usually placed before a direct object.

8. The girl lent her new typewriter to her friend.

_____

9. She is teaching geography to the students.

_____

10. Don't mention this matter to your friends.

_____

11. He had time to speak only a few words to his children.

_____

12. He said nothing to me at the time.

_____

13. Next time I will write a longer letter to you.

_____

14. I must recommend a wonderful restaurant to you.

_____

15. May I suggest something to you?

_____

16. We gave it to her.[3]

_____

17. They submitted their bid to the government.

_____

18. He told the story to his brother.

_____

19. He said something to his brother.

_____

20. Can you recommend a good grammar book to us?

_____

21. Please explain the meaning of this word to me.

_____

[3] If both objects are personal pronouns, American usage permits only the **to** indirect object.

8-6
PREPOSITIONS AFTER ADJECTIVES

Many adjectives are followed by prepositions.

from	absent, different, distinct, remote
for	enough, fit, good, grateful, necessary, responsible
in	deficient, proficient, successful
with	compatible, consistent, content, gentle, patient
(up)on	dependent, intent
about	careful (*or* of), enthusiastic (*or* over), happy
of	afraid, aware, certain, conscious, critical, deserving, desirous, envious, fearful, fond, full, glad, guilty, ignorant, innocent, jealous, positive, proud, thoughtful, tolerant, worthy
to	acceptable, adjacent, attentive, beneficial, detrimental, essential, faithful, friendly, generous, hostile, inferior, kind, obedient, painful, partial, polite, preferable, rude, similar

Use the required preposition after each adjective.

1. He is frequently absent _____ school because of illness.

2. All that equipment is not necessary _____ our experiment.

3. He is very proficient _____ English, but very deficient _____ mathematics.

4. We'll have to be content _____ the few supplies we have.

5. The young man left home because he no longer wanted to be dependent _____ his parents.

6. He was quite aware _____ the appeal he had for women.

7. That proposal is not acceptable _____ our company.

8. He has always been faithful _____ his wife.

9. He is quite different _____ his brother.[4]

10. We're very grateful to you _____ all your help.

11. He has never been successful _____ anything he has under-taken.

12. He's very critical _____ everyone but himself.

13. How thoughtful _____ you to send flowers to the old lady in the hospital.

14. The cemetery is adjacent _____ the church.

15. Too much smoking or drinking is detrimental _____ the health.

16. Is the paper bag strong enough _____ this carton of milk?

[4]The conjunction **than** may also be heard informally after **different**.

17. Although he's a stern, gruff man, he's very gentle _____ children.

18. He's not enthusiastic _____ his new job.

19. She's very fond _____ young children.

20. He is very attentive _____ all pretty women.

21. The jury decided the defendant was guilty _____ the murder he was accused of.

22. She is responsible _____ all the supplies that are distributed.

23. He always tries to be polite _____ his elders.

24. She's very jealous _____ the attention her younger sister gets.

25. She has always felt inferior _____ her husband.

26. I'm proud _____ the way you behaved in that difficult situation.

27. You must be very careful _____ what you say to him.

8-7
PREPOSITIONS AFTER PARTICIPIAL ADJECTIVES

Many **-ed** participial adjectives are followed by prepositions, usually **in, to, with, at, about** or **over, by, of.**

> I'm tired of his never-ending complaints.
> They have been blessed with many children.
> We are alarmed at (or by) the way the children have been behaving recently.

At or **by** frequently follows **-ed** participial adjectives expressing emotion. **By** after **-ed** adjectives usually strengthens the passive force of these participial forms.

Use the required preposition. In some cases two prepositions are possible.

1. He was so absorbed _____ the work he was doing that he didn't notice our entrance into the room.

2. I'm well acquainted _____ the situation you're referring to.

3. Late in life he was afflicted _____ a terrible disease.

4. I'm not ashamed _____ anything I've done.

5. Astonished _____ what he saw, he stood rooted to the spot.

6. Water is composed _____ hydrogen and oxygen.

7. I'm quite concerned _____ the health of my wife.

8. He is endowed _____ very great gifts.

9. Embarrassed _____ the many compliments he was receiving, the explorer began to wish he could leave the room.

10. We're all impressed _____ your great knowledge of the subject.

11. I'm interested _____ buying a diamond ring for my wife.

12. Pleased _____ the impression he was making, he began to tell about another one of his adventures.

13. Because of the way his wife has behaved, he is disillusioned _____ all women.

14. We were all shocked _____ the way they had been treating the children.

15. He's satisfied _____ the car he has just bought.

8-8
VERB-PREPOSITION COMBINATIONS (1)

Many idioms consist of common one-syllable verbs plus prepositions.

bring	about		*cause*	give	up		*surrender, relinquish*
	up		*raise a subject, rear*		out		*distribute*
call	up		*telephone*	go	over	NS	*review, rehearse*
	(up)on	NS[5]	*visit*		with	NS	*date*
	off		*cancel*	hand	in		*submit*
come	up	NS	*arise*		down		*transmit*
do	without	NS	*sacrifice, not need*	hold	up		*rob*
get	up	NS	*wake up, awake*		down		*suppress*
	over	NS	*recover from*				

Use the appropriate prepositional form.

1. The soldiers gave _____ (surrendered) after a hard battle.

2. I wonder what brought _____ (caused) his strange behavior?

3. The meeting has been called _____ (canceled) because some of the members are ill.

4. He feels that he can do _____ (not need) many of the luxuries he now has.

5. A man was giving _____ (distributing) leaflets at the entrance to the hall.

6. Jane is going _____ (dating) a very fine young man now.

[5]NS = nonseparable. See exercise 8-11.

7. The man who held _____ (robbed) the bank was caught soon after.

8. This question has been brought _____ (raised) again and again at the committee meeetings.

9. Call _____ (telephone) your friend and invite him to come with us.

10. He doesn't like to get _____ (awake) while it's still dark.

11. Let's go _____ (review) the next lesson together.

12. This ring has been handed _____ (transmitted) from generation to generation.

13. He is being brought _____ (raised) to be a gentleman.

14. A problem has come _____ (arisen) that requires our immediate attention.

15. I can't seem to get _____ (recover from) this cold.

16. All applications should be handed _____ (submitted) right away.

17. These people are too proud and independent to be held _____ (suppressed) for long.

18. A good traveling salesman calls _____ (visits) all his customers as often as he can.

8-9

VERB-PREPOSITION COMBINATIONS (2)

keep	on	NS	*continue*	put	off		*postpone*
	off	NS	*refrain from going on*		on		*don (clothes)*
					out		*extinguish*
look	after	NS	*take care of*	run	across	NS	*meet or find by chance (also* come across*)*
	up		*search for information*				
make	out		*understand*		over	NS	*(get) hit by a car*
	up	NS	*become reconciled, invent*	take	after	NS	*resemble*
					over		*assume control*
pass	out	NS	*distribute*		up		*consider, discuss*
		NS	*faint*		off		*remove (clothes)*
pick	out		*select*	turn	down		*reject*
	up		*come to get*		off		*stop some kind of power*
					on		*start some kind of power*
					up	NS	*appear*

Use the appropriate prepositional form.

1. You can look _____ (search for) the information you want in any encyclopedia.

2. If we don't get more air in this room, I'll pass _____ (faint) from the heat.

3. They couldn't have picked _____ (selected) a better site for the home they are planning to build.

4. No smoking is allowed here. Please put _____ (extinguish) your cigarette.

5. This intersection near the school is very dangerous. Several children have been run _____ (hit by cars) here.

6. There are several more questions we must take _____ (consider) before we adjourn the meeting.

7. As soon as he entered the house he turned _____ (stopped the electricity) the porch light and turned _____ (start the electricity) the hall light.

8. You will be criticized if you don't turn _____ (appear) for that meeting.

9. Anyone who keeps _____ (continues) making the same mistakes is not very intelligent.

10. I can't make _____ (understand) whether this letter is a *p* or a *q*.

11. Never put _____ (postpone) for tomorrow what you can do today.

12. The girl is very beautiful; she takes _____ (resembles) her mother.

13. She turned _____ (rejected) his offer of marriage.

14. Can't you see that the sign says, "Keep _____ (refrain from going on) the grass?

15. Now that they're divorced, who is looking _____ (taking care of) the children?

16. They had a bitter quarrel, and they never made _____ (became reconciled) after that.

17. He is putting _____ (donning) his oldest clothes to paint the house.

18. While she was cleaning the attic she ran _____ (found by chance) some letters she thought she had destroyed years ago.

19. During the revolution, the rebels took _____ (assumed control of) all the radio stations.

20. All the test papers have already been passed _____ (distributed).

21. The laundryman will pick _____ (come to get) the laundry in the morning.

22. They had to put _____ (postpone) their vocation because one of their children became ill.

8-10
VERB-PREPOSITION COMBINATIONS (3)
(REVIEW)

Use the verb-preposition combination that is the equivalent of the word(s) in parentheses.

1. The soldiers refused to _____ (surrender).

2. He was _____ (raised) in a tiny village.

3. I shall be very pleased to have you _____ (visit) me.

4. I hope the football game won't have to be _____ (canceled) because of the rainy weather.

5. We need to provide for any unexpected difficulties that might _____ (arise).

6. He was able to _____ (submit) his report before it was actually due.

7. In an unlimited monarchy, the ruling power is _____ (transmitted) to someone in the royal family.

8. Crime in the streets is getting so bad that a thief will _____ (rob) a person in broad daylight.

9. If you _____ (continue) spending money like that, you'll soon have none left.

10. He is the kind of person who _____ (appears) when he is least expected.

11. Those stories he _____ (invents) about his past exploits are delightful.

12. The tie he has _____ (selected) goes very well with his suit.

13. A procrastinator likes to _____ (postpone) doing the things that should be done right away.

14. We _____ (remove) our coats and hats when we enter a house.

15. The prepositions are being _____ (considered) this week.

8-11
SEPARABLE VERBS

A number of verb-preposition combinations permit a short object to come between their two parts.

He called up *his wife*.

or   He called *his wife* up.

If the object is a personal pronoun, it must come between the two parts of the verb.

He called *her* up.

With other verb-preposition combinations, the object appears only after the prepositional form.

He'll call on **his new customers** tomorrow.
He'll call on **them** tomorrow.

These nonseparable verbs have been marked NS in the preceding exercises (Nos. 8-8 and 8-9). The other verbs listed there are separable if they are transitive.

Use the required pronoun and the proper form of the verb-preposition combination.

EXAMPLE: a. Aren't you going to *the meeting*? No, they've ___called___ ___it___ ___off___ . (canceled) (**Call off** is a separable verb.)

b. *These lessons* are difficult. Let's ___go___ ___over___ ___them___ (review) together. (**Go over** is a nonseparable verb.)

1. I'd better see *the doctor* about this infection. I'll _____ _____ _____ (telephone) right away.

2. The typist has had *the flu* for a long time but she has finally _____ _____ _____ (recovered from) and is back in the office.

3. Aren't they living in *their apartment* on Smith Street? No, they _____ _____ (relinquished) last year and moved into a large house.

4. Here are *some good books* on the subject. Please _____ _____ (select). (Use **one**)[6]

5. *The articles* are very difficult to learn. We will _____ _____ _____ (consider) next week.

6. Was *their bid for the contract* accepted? No, the company _____ _____ (rejected) because it was too high.

7. Here's *an interesting article* about your country. I just _____ _____ (found by chance) in a magazine.

8. How does *this airconditioner* work? I would like to _____ _____ (start)

9. Do you want to get *a car* for your teen-age son? No, he can _____ _____ (not need) for a while longer. (Use **one**)

10. Here are *your rubbers*. Please _____ _____ _____ (don)

11. *The books* have finally been delivered. We'll _____ _____ (distribute) tomorrow.

[6]Some pronouns like **one, this, some** may come before or after the prepositional form in a separable verb.

12. We can't hold *the meeting* tonight. We'll have to _____

_____ _____ (postpone) until

tomorrow.

13. *My new shoes* are hurting me. I'm going to _____ _____

_____ _____ (remove) for a while.

14. *Their art teacher* had planned a trip to the museum, but he had to _____

_____ _____ (cancel)

because he became ill.

8-12

PASSIVE OF VERB + PREPOSITION COMBINATIONS

Rewrite the following sentences, changing the italicized verb + preposition combinations to the passive voice. Do not use a **by** phrase if the sentences begins with **they** or **people**.

EXAMPLE: a. Their aunt and uncle *brought up* the orphaned children.
   The orphaned children were brought up by their aunt and uncle. _____
   (Note that the preposition remains with the verb.)
   b. They may call off the lecture series if they don't sell enough tickets.
   The lecture series may be called off if they don't sell enough tickets. _____

1. The campaign workers *were handing out* leaflets at the meeting.

_____

2. The company *turned off* his electricity because he had not paid his bills.

_____

_____

3. The robbers *had disposed of* the stolen goods before the police arrested them.

_____

_____

4. The students *will have handed in* many reports before the end of the year.

_____

_____

5. They *must decide on* a new plan soon.

_____

6. He is a man whom they *can count on*.

_____

7. People *should try on* clothes before they *buy* them. (two passives)

_____

8. They *held up* our bank last night.

_____

9. The fairy tales which the kindergarten teacher *made up* for the children were very charming.

_____

_____

10. People *will make fun of* you if you give such a silly speech.

_____

11. People always *take advantage of* him because he is so naive.

_____

12. We *must take up* that matter at our next meeting.

_____

13. They *blew up* the bridge after they retreated from the enemy.

_____

14. One of the students *is giving out* the examination papers.

_____

15. They *turned down* the bid because it was too high.

_____

16. Her aunt *is taking care of* her.

_____

17. They *will operate on* him tomorrow.

_____

18. People *have* really *taken notice of* him since he published his book.

_____

8-13
PHRASAL PREPOSITIONS

Prepositions may consist of two or three parts.

1. Two parts—**because of, along with, according to, apart from, owing to, as for, short of, instead of, ahead of, regardless of, contrary to, prior to, subject to.**
2. Three parts—**by way of, in spite of, with (or in) regard to, in addition to, in (the) back of (or at the back of), by means of, for fear of, for the sake of, on account of, on behalf of, as a result of, in return for, in accordance with, with (or in) reference to, in favor of, in connection with, as well as, on the point of.**

Supply the missing parts of the phrasal prepositions.

1. The train arrived ahead _____ schedule.

2. Instead _____ listening to his parents, he did just as he pleased.

3. Regardless _____ the consequences, he went ahead with his foolhardy plan.

4. According _____ the newspapers, the President will arrive next week.

5. I don't know what decisions others may make, but as _____ me, give me liberty or give me death.

6. Owing _____ a mistake made by the computer, he received a check for one million dollars.

7. The prices quoted are subject _____ change without notice.

8. Prior _____ his marriage, he had spent money very foolishly.

9. We're very short _____ paper; please order some more immediately.

10. Contrary _____ expectations, the young boy did very well on the examinations.

11. Apart _____ his parents, no one knew that he was planning to leave the country.

12. They were just _____ the point _____ leaving the house when some unexpected visitors arrived.

13. He became paralyzed _____ a result _____ a stroke he had had recently.

14. _____ accordance _____ your request, we are canceling your magazine subscription.

15. All the campaign workers were given handsome gifts _____ return _____ their help.

16. The students sitting _____ the back _____ the room could barely hear the professor.

17. _____ behalf _____ the citizens of his town, the mayor gave his distinguished visitor the keys of the city.

18. _____ the sake _____ peace in the family, she never argued with her husband.

19. Many problems have arisen _____ connection _____ the construction of the new library.

20. The teacher, _____ well _____ the students, was disappointed at the cancellation of their camping trip.

21. _____ means _____ hard work, the young man quickly climbed to the highest position in his department.

22. _____ reference _____ your recent letter, we wish to state that your order is being sent out next week.

Prepositional phrases can be the equivalent of adverbial clauses, especially those phrases beginning with **because of, in spite of, in case of**.

Change the italicized clauses to prepositional phrases.

EXAMPLE: a. *Because he was careless*, he lost his job.
Because of his carelessness, he lost his job.

b. *Although he is blind*, he manages to live a normal life.
In spite of his blindness (or despite his blindness), he manages to live a normal life.

c. *If there is an accident*, notify the police at once.
In case of an accident (or in the event of an accident), notify the police at once.

1. *Because he is selfish*, he has very few friends.

2. *Although he is young*, he assumes great responsibility.

3. *If there is a strike*, all production will be halted.

4. *Because he was injured*, an ambulance had to be called for.

5. *Although they were poor*, they managed to furnish their apartment in good taste.

6. *Because they were lonely in the city*, they moved back to the country.

7. *Although he is bad-tempered*, he is really a kind person.

8. *If there is a cancellation*, we will let you know at once.

9. He was rewarded *because he was loyal to his king*.

10. *Although she was ill*, she came to work.

_____

11. *If the weather is bad*, the picnic will be postponed.

_____

12. *Although he was innocent*, the jury declared him guilty.

_____

8-15
LIKE, AS

Like and **as** often express comparison or manner.

Comparison	***Like his father***, he loves to go hunting and fishing. This tea is (as) cold *as* ice.
Manner (*may be* *related to* *comparison*)	He has always behaved *like* a perfect gentleman. But—If a verb follows **gentleman,** formal usage requires the conjunction **as**— *He has always behaved **as** a gentleman should* (*behave*).

Like and **as** (usually **such as**) may be used to cite an example—**Fruits like** (or **such as**) **apples and bananas are often used for dessert.**

The preposition **as** may also occur in many other types of sentences.

He demanded his rights *as* a citizen.
The teacher appointed a student to act *as* monitor until she returned. (**as** = in the capacity of)
In biology, the horse is classified *as* a mammal.
We regard him *as* the best possible candidate.

Supply **like** or **as**. Follow formal usage.

1. At school, the young prince wanted to be treated _____ everyone else.

2. _____ a young man, he was very energetic and quick.

3. She is not so cooperative _____ her sister is.

4. She is not cooperative _____ her sister.

5. A sick man _____ him shouldn't work so hard.

6. The dictionary defines democracy _____ "government by the people."

7. People used to say that Stalin was as hard _____ steel.

8. Don't ask questions. Please do _____ you are told.

9. She looks just _____ her mother.

10. The rumor spread _____ wildfire throughout the school.

11. He has been described _____ a very honest and loyal official.

12. The men were asked to select the bravest amongst them _____ their leader.

13. Flowers _____ orchids and gardenias grow only in warm climates.

14. She refers to herself _____ the queen of the kitchen.

15. An opportunity _____ this doesn't present itself every day.

16. He is regarded _____ a saint by many of his followers.

17. Sometimes his secretary dresses _____ a movie star.

18. The Vice President must function _____ the head of the government if anything happens to the President.

19. He has a habit of classifying everyone he meets _____ a friend or _____ an enemy.

20. He often acts _____ a man who is not in his right mind.

8-16
PREPOSITIONS
IN ADVERBIAL WORD GROUPS

Prepositions are often used in adverbial word groups. In such adverbials, countable nouns may occur without articles—**for example, by accident, in fact**. Also, adjective forms may function as the objects of prepositions—**for good, at first, in general**.

Supply the proper prepositions for each adverbial word group.

1. They had a bitter quarrel about the money. _____ the end, they decided to divide it equally.

2. All these rugs are made _____ hand.

3. He has left the country _____ good. He will never return.

4. He made a few mistakes, but _____ the whole, I think he did a good job.

5. All payments must be made _____ advance.

6. The young boy learned very fast, and _____ due course he became president of the company.

7. Do you think she hurt his feelings _____ purpose?

8. _____ accident, she stepped into a deep puddle of water.

9. Surrounded by the enemy _____ all sides, they had no choice but to surrender.

10. _____ chance, do you remember where they live?

11. We'll have to walk. The elevator is _____ _____ order.

12. There will be twenty guests _____ all.

13. He is _____ far the worst student in the class.

14. She has no patience with children _____ all.

15. This package was left here _____ mistake.

16. She loves bargains. She's going to look at some dresses that are _____ sale downtown.

17. Several houses in the area are _____ sale.

18. To memorize means to learn _____ heart.

19. His complaint is about the policy of the company _____ general, not about any one person _____ particular.

20. She was on the phone for a long time; _____ the meantime her dinner was burning on the stove.

21. _____ the one hand he would like to spend the summer writing his book. _____ the other hand, he feels that he ought to travel during his vacation.

22. _____ occasion he wonders why he accepted the new job. _____ a matter _____ fact he thinks he made a mistake altogether in accepting it.

23. _____ a rule, he goes to bed at 10 o'clock. _____ fact, he has rarely gone to bed later than 11 o'clock.

Appendix

Simple Form of the Verb	Past Tense	Past Participle
abide (*literary*)	abode	abode
arise	arose	arisen
awake	awoke (*sometimes* awaked)	awaked (*Brit.* awoke, awoken)
be	was	been
bear	bore	borne (*meaning* carry)
		born (*meaning* have children)
beat	beat	beaten (*sometimes* beat)
become	became	become
begin	began	begun
behold	beheld	beheld
bend	bent	bent
beseech (*literary*)	besought (*or* beseeched)	besought (*or* beseeched)
bet	bet (*sometimes* betted)	bet (*sometimes* betted)
bid (*meaning* offer money at an auction)	bid	bid
bid (*meaning* ask someone to do something)	bade (*or* bid)	bidden (*or* bid)
bind	bound	bound
bite	bit	bitten (*or* bit)
bleed	bled	bled
blow	blew	blown
break	broke	broken
breed	bred	bred
bring	brought	brought
broadcast	broadcast (*sometimes* broadcasted)	broadcast (*sometimes* broadcasted)
build	built	built
burst	burst	burst
buy	bought	bought
cast	cast	cast
catch	caught	caught
chide	chid (*also* chided)	chidden (*also* chided)
choose	chose	chosen

Simple Form of the Verb	Past Tense	Past Participle
cling	clung	clung
clothe	clad (*literary*) (*also* clothed)	clad (*literary*) (*also* clothed)
come	came	come
cost	cost	cost
creep	crept	crept
dig	dug	dug
do	did	done
draw	drew	drawn
dream	dreamt (*more often* dreamed)	dreamt (*more often* dreamed)
drink	drank	drunk
drive	drove	driven
eat	ate	eaten
fall	fell	fallen
feed	fed	fed
feel	felt	felt
fight	fought	fought
find	found	found
flee	fled	fled
fling	flung	flung
fly	flew	flown
forbid	forbade (*or* forbad)	forbidden
forget	forgot	forgotten (*Brit.* forgot)
forsake	forsook	forsaken
freeze	froze	frozen
get	got	gotten (*Brit.* got)
go	went	gone
grind	ground	ground
grow	grew	grown
hang	hung / hanged (*meaning* suspended by the neck)	hung / hanged (*meaning* suspended by the neck)
have	had	had
hear	heard	heard
hide	hid	hidden
hit	hit	hit
hold	held	held
hurt	hurt	hurt
keep	kept	kept
kneel	knelt (*or* kneeled)	knelt (*or* kneeled)
knit	knit (*or* knitted)	knit (*or* knitted)
know	knew	known
lay	laid	laid
lead	led	led
leap	lept (*more often* leaped)	lept (*more often* leaped)
leave	left	left
lend	lent	lent
let	let	let
lie	lay	lain
light	lit (*more often* lighted)	lit (*more often* lighted)
lose	lost	lost
make	made	made
mean	meant	meant
meet	met	met
mislay	mislaid	mislaid
mistake	mistook	mistaken

Simple Form of the Verb	Past Tense	Past Participle
overcome	overcame	overcome
pay	paid	paid
put	put	put
read	read	read
rend	rent	rent
rid	rid	rid
ride	rode	ridden
ring	rang	rung
rise	rose	risen
run	ran	run
say	said	said
see	saw	seen
seek	sought	sought
sell	sold	sold
send	sent	sent
set	set	set
shake	shook	shaken
shed	shed	shed
shine (*intrans.*)	shone	shone
shoe	shod (*or* shoed)	shod (*or* shoed, shodden)
shoot	shot	shot
show	showed	shown (*or* showed)
shrink	shrank (*also* shrunk)	shrunk
shut	shut	shut
sing	sang	sung
sink	sank (*also* sunk)	sunk
sit	sat	sat
sleep	slept	slept
slide	slid	slid
sling	slung	slung
slink	slunk	slunk
slit	slit	slit
smite	smote	smitten
speak	spoke	spoken
speed	sped (*or* speeded)	sped (*or* speeded)
spend	spent	spent
spin	spun	spun
spit	spit (*sometimes* spat)	spit (*sometimes* spat)
split	split	split
spread	spread	spread
spring	sprang (*also* sprung)	sprung
stand	stood	stood
steal	stole	stolen
stick	stuck	stuck
sting	stung	stung
stink	stank	stunk
strew	strewed	strewn (*or* strewed)
stride	strode	stridden
strike	struck	struck
string	strung	strung
strive	strove (*also* strived)	striven (*also* strived)
swear	swore	sworn
sweep	swept	swept
swim	swam	swum
swing	swung	swung

Simple Form of the Verb	Past Tense	Past Participle
take	took	taken
teach	taught	taught
tear	tore	torn
tell	told	told
think	thought	thought
throw	threw	thrown
thrive	throve (*or* thrived)	thriven (*or* thrived)
thrust	thrust	thrust
tread (*literary*)	trod	trodden (*or* trod)
undergo	underwent	undergone
understand	understood	understood
wake	woke (*sometimes* waked)	waked (*Brit.* woke, woken)
wear	wore	worn
weave	wove	woven
weep	wept	wept
win	won	won
wind	wound	wound
withdraw	withdrew	withdrawn
withhold	withheld	withheld
withstand	withstood	withstood
wring	wrung	wrung
write	wrote	written